ON POETRY AND POLITICS

On Poetry and Politics

Jean Paulhan

Edited and with an Introduction
by Jennifer Bajorek and Eric Trudel

Translated from the French
by Jennifer Bajorek, Charlotte Mandell,
and Eric Trudel

University of Illinois Press
Urbana and Chicago

Manufactured in the United States of America
C 5 4 3 2 1

∞ This book is printed on acid-free paper.

Library of Congress Cataloging-in-Publication Data

Paulhan, Jean, 1884–1968.
On poetry and politics / Jean Paulhan ; edited and with an introduction by Jennifer Bajorek and Eric Trudel ; translated from the French by Jennifer Bajorek, Charlotte Mandell, and Eric Trudel.
p. cm.
Includes bibliographical references and index.
ISBN-13 978-0-252-03280-6 (cloth : alk. paper)
ISBN-10 0-252-03280-2 (cloth : alk. paper)
1. Literature—History and criticism. 2. Literature—Philosophy. 3. History, Modern—20th century.
I. Bajorek, Jennifer. II. Trudel, Eric.
III. Mandell, Charlotte. IV. Title.
PN513.P38 2008
848'.912—dc22 2007045203

CONTENTS

INTRODUCTION

Jennifer Bajorek and Eric Trudel

Anglophone readers who recognize Jean Paulhan's name are likely to associate it with two phrases: first, the title of the highly influential journal whose editorial direction Paulhan assumed in 1925 and carried for many years thereafter, the *Nouvelle Revue Française* (hereafter *NRF*); second, the period descriptor *l'entre-deux-guerres*, frequently attached to that same journal in order to mark the span of its proverbial long shadow in French intellectual history.

This volume aims to expand and, in certain instances, to explode these associations in favor of a larger Paulhan. With these selections and translations, we seek to show both man and work as speaking to a much broader set of concerns than could ever be exhausted by a single publishing program, no matter how eclectic, politically committed, or intellectually luminous, or by a single set of wars, no matter how far reaching and determining its consequences with respect to our own moment. After all, we are living in a time in which it makes less and less sense to talk about "two wars," in France or anywhere else. We believe, and all of the texts collected here attest, that Paulhan has something extraordinary to offer us today, not only as an editor (whose inimitable eye, ear, and mind and courageous decisions are now, thankfully, well documented in English as well as French),[1] but as a literary theorist, cultural critic, and social and political commentator. That is to say, perhaps above all, that Paulhan has something extraordinary to offer us today as a writer, whether his explicit topic is poetry or politics.

There is something about the writer's task that, for Paulhan, is common to us all, as the texts collected here repeatedly expose. That this task is common in yet another sense, born of our everyday engagement with the opacities and resistances of language, in no way diminishes its exemplarity. On the contrary, it sheds light on our engagement with language as the everyday element of our existence as human or, at least, as *thinking*, beings. The texts collected here illuminate, in their way, these opacities and resistances. All of them demonstrate an intensity of engagement, with language and with thought that was, for Paulhan, in no way diminished by its everyday character. As the reader of this volume will quickly discover, Paulhan had a habit of underscoring those aspects of his theories that were, precisely, banal, even as he succeeded in investing them with a sense of mystery, joy, and adventure.

If language is exemplary and a common topic here, however, it is not at the expense of a whole host of other themes and problems: democracy, resistance, peace; Terror and terrorists; the principles of jury selection; the arbitrariness of the borders of Europe and the limitations of its definitions of citizenship, homelands, and patriotism; what it feels like to fly in an airplane for the first time, to speak a foreign tongue, or to misconstrue the thing we are holding in our hand; what it feels like to be in love, to have a body, to be duped by an advertisement.

This list, drawn from the contents of this volume, whose dates of composition and original publication span the years 1913 to 1951, bears witness to the striking diversity of Paulhan's projects. For all their diversity, they are not unconnected with one another, and it is in these connections that we can begin to discern, as we have already suggested, the singular contours of Paulhan's concerns and turn of mind. The passage about flying is also a passage about Europe: about the failure of the Council of Europe that met in Strasbourg in the autumn of 1949 to "bear any resemblance to Europe" ("Letter to the Directors about Europe"). Among the sometimes startling descriptions of embodiment are those that evoke the experience of the German occupation, which, we are told, differs from that of dancing or wearing ribbons but can perhaps be grasped as a way of moving through the street: a willingness—or unwillingness—to pick up the package a passerby has dropped ("The Bee"). And then there is the patriot's desire to hold his country in his hand: what it turns out can be rather difficult in the case of a colonial and even postcolonial France "so vast and so complicated that it spills over into Africa and Asia" ("Letter to the Directors about Europe"). Finally, there are the complex insights to be drawn from the simple observation that our eyes are on the front of our head: "A man can no more grasp his mind *intact* than he can directly see the nape of his neck or his throat. There are, however, mirrors for seeing the back and front of the neck. But there are none for the mind" ("Young Lady with Mirrors"). In more than one of the texts collected here, Paulhan not only draws these insights but does not hesitate to flesh them out in some of their most challenging implications, which are not simply linguistic but ethical as well as philosophical.

Michael Syrotinski, in a recent volume of new scholarship on Paulhan, characterizes his work as grappling with "a certain otherness of language," constantly asking how language can take us "to its edge and beyond, whether this is formulated as the real, materiality, an event, or the singularity of experience."[2] The singularity of *this* experience—of grasping that our thoughts are made of language and thus not mirrored by it—is expressed through what Paulhan calls, in "Rhetoric Rises from Its Ashes," "a rhetorical event." The event is almost always unexpected but also common; it is thoroughly metaphorical, it turns on a metaphor, but at the same time is startlingly material. One consequence of the mirror metaphor, as of Paulhan's larger theories of language, is that we, as beings who would reflect on our own minds, have no choice but to engage with a language that is connected not only with rhetoric but with literature and poetry. This brings us to a short description of this volume's first section.[3]

ON POETRY AND PROVERBS

The first text translated here, "The Experience of the Proverb," gives the reader a slice of one of Paulhan's first major projects. Written in 1913 and revised more than once before it was finally published in 1925, the essay is, broadly speaking, ethnographic in intention, together with his collection and translation of the Malagasy *hain-teny* (*Les Hain-Teny Mérinas. Poésies populaires malgaches)* (Paris: Librairie orientaliste Geuthner, 1913) (The Merina Hain-Teny: Malagasy Popular Poetry); the short text entitled *Le Repas et l'amour chez les Mérinas* (Montpellier: Fata Morgana, 1970) (Meals and Love among the Merina); and "The Semantics of the Proverb," a doctoral dissertation in progress for more than twenty-five years but never completed.[4] Its central themes already give rise to observations anticipating, in broad strokes, Paulhan's more general theories of language and point toward the major concerns of his later texts on rhetoric and poetry. In fact, Paulhan's early fascination with proverbs, figures, and other "events" of language—and his fascination, above all, with the commonplace expression (*lieu commun*), which arguably constitutes the theoretical matrix of his later writings—first takes shape in colonial Madagascar. There he spent three years, from 1908 to 1910, as a secondary-school teacher among the Hova (or Merina). The same could be said for the utopian horizon toward which his work in some sense always tended.

In Madagascar, Paulhan witnessed and eventually became proficient in a kind of ritualized oratory and poetic jousting, in which proverbs (the *hain-teny*) are traded until the authority of one utterance suddenly gains the assent of all involved and brings the exchange to a close. According to Paulhan, the name *hain-teny* "can mean both 'science of language,' or 'science of words'; also 'learned words' and, if you put a little pressure on it, 'wise words.'"[5] Paulhan collects, translates, and at first tries to understand these enigmatic *hain-teny* by classifying them thematically: love, pride, social interaction, morals, and so forth. This careful, methodical approach turns out to be inadequate, however, and Paulhan quickly becomes convinced that the *hain-teny* hold a secret and a greater promise, seeming to reveal a superior order of reality, distinct from common sentences, in which meaning is granted with the force and immediacy of the obvious.

"The Experience of the Proverb" documents this shift in perspective. In it, Paulhan tells the tale of his failure to gain any satisfactory scientific knowledge or understanding of these proverbs. As the text explains, as long as he tries to grasp the meaning of a proverb, scrutinizing its theme, its motifs, its syntax, or even what he assumes to be its lesson, he remains incapable of making effective use of it. As soon as he utters it with blind conviction or without anxiety, however, the event of language occurs, and the proverb "works." Paulhan will constantly return to these felicities of expression, and the Madagascans' use of proverbs will remain, for him, the very model of a functional Rhetoric, free of Terror.

This twinned reference, to Rhetoric and Terror, brings us to the next four essays, dealing with language, rhetoric, and poetry at a more sustained theoretical level. Although these texts can (and, we want to suggest, should) be read for their own sake, they are all intimately related to Paulhan's most famous book and contribution to twentieth-century literary theory, *Les Fleurs de Tarbes, ou, La Terreur dans les lettres* (Paris: Gallimard, 1941) (*The Flowers of Tarbes, or, Terror in Literature,* trans. Michael Syrotinski) (Urbana: University of Illinois Press, 2006). (An earlier version appeared serially in the *NRF* in 1936.) This book is, at least on one reading, an attempt to rehabilitate rhetoric and the arts of language, over and against the claims made for an artless, direct, and unmediated presentation of things as they are.

In two of the texts related to this project—"Rhetoric Rises from Its Ashes" and "Young Lady with Mirrors," both published in 1938—Paulhan challenges what he calls "Terror," the violent rejection of form and words, and the dream (it is at once a hope and a sorry delusion) of a perfect transparency of expression. The terrorist believes that "the presence of the commonplace expression betrays servitude and submission at every turn" ("Rhetoric Rises from Its Ashes") and that "language is essentially dangerous for thought."[6] We might be tempted to imagine that Paulhan will advocate, against this Terror, a *return* to Rhetoric, an acceptance of rules and commonplace expressions and a kind of confidence in language "itself." But, as readers of this deceptively simple text quickly learn, things are not so clear-cut, and Paulhan shows the conflict between Terror and Rhetoric to be without the desired resolution: Terror, pushed to its logical conclusion, ends by reestablishing the very prison of language it was seeking to avoid, whereas Rhetoric's sway over our minds and thoughts continually runs the risk of tyranny. Paulhan speaks more than once in these pages of a "freedom of the mind" that is threatened by Rhetoric.

It is significant that, upon his return from Madagascar and after the First World War (in which he fought and was wounded), Paulhan rubbed shoulders with dada and then with surrealism—two movements whose authors and works later came, for Paulhan, to be arbiters of Terror. In Max Ernst's famous painting *Le Rendez-vous des amis* (1922), Paulhan can be seen sitting among André Breton, Paul Éluard, Louis Aragon, Philippe Soupault, and Jean Arp. Another indication of the surrealist company Paulhan kept is that the earliest of the four essays of literary theory included in this volume—"Jacob Cow the Pirate, or, If Words Are Signs"—was first published, in 1920, in three successive issues of *Littérature,* the journal edited by Breton, Soupault, and Aragon. But we risk a misunderstanding here: if "Jacob Cow" can be construed as expressing an undeniable mistrust of language and serious doubts about its capacity to make sense, then Paulhan's interest in the arbitrariness of words, his close scrutiny of the impossibility of ever telling words and ideas apart, and his (tongue-in-cheek) critique of the belief in words' dangerous power over thought can all be understood to anticipate his denunciation of Terror.

Last among the texts of literary theory collected here is "Key to Poetry," completed in 1944 and considered by Paulhan to be a kind of supplement to *The Flowers of Tarbes*. In this text, as its title suggests, Paulhan proposes to define, elaborate, and demonstrate, with "mathematical precision,"[7] a universal law of poetic mystery. In a reversal typical of

Paulhan's thought (similar to the one we saw in "The Experience of the Proverb"), the very moment in which Paulhan's text attempts finally to grasp and enunciate, after long and methodical effort, the "key," is at the same time a performative moment in which the literary theorist's own discourse is exceeded, blinded by, and becomes the very thing it was until then seeking to isolate and define: what Paulhan says he has no choice but to call "poetry." Indeed, despite Paulhan's frequent claims to have achieved a rigorous and methodical view of the literary phenomenon (in his correspondence, he often compares *The Flowers of Tarbes* to a new *Discourse on Method*), and despite his professed determination *not* to make the essence or nature of literature into a strict impossibility, every one of his essays on rhetoric and on language follows the same path, in which the result of all this methodical effort and research turns out to be, at the same time and necessarily, its own dismantling or falling short.

This reversal begets two further highly idiosyncratic gestures: one is this tendency of Paulhan's texts to recall the modesty of their purpose; the other is this tendency for them to call on their reader, and to call for his (or her) participation. In "Key to Poetry," for example, Paulhan addresses his reader directly: "Here however, it is no longer my task . . . but my reader's (yes, I am talking to you), if you have had the extraordinary patience to follow me, and to find yourself, suddenly, transformed." These gestures crop up again in the so-called political writings, where they entail a shift, if not necessarily an increase, in stakes.

ON POLITICS AND RESISTANCE

For all their connections with the texts on language, rhetoric, and poetry, Paulhan's political writings can seem, even to readers of the former, strikingly original and unsettling. Whether written in the thick of war or in its margins—"Democracy Calls on the First to Come Along" was written in 1939; "The Bee" was written and published in *Les Cahiers de la Libération* in February 1944; the three "Letters," "Letter on Peace," "Letter to the Directors about Europe," and "Letter to the Directors of the Resistance," were all written in 1949—these texts are remarkable for their peculiar perspicacity stemming less from any one position they take, with regard to any one historical circumstance or personal or collective experience, than from their ability to destabilize and rework the relations between these things. All of the old ingredients in the pie of politics are rendered labile and open to revision.

This is not to say that Paulhan's political writings do not also take positions. They do indeed take them, and no introduction to Paulhan's political writings would be complete without at least mentioning the intensely *engagé* nature of Paulhan's wartime activities. A Résistant among Résistants, Paulhan brought publication of the *NRF* to a halt at the start of the German occupation, publishing a final issue in June 1940, and immediately transferred his editorial and publishing expertise to the cause of the Resistance.[8] One scholar recently dubbed Paulhan the "director" of the literary and publishing arm of the Resistance, playing on his title as an editorial director and echoing the title of the closing "Letter" in our sequence. In "The Bee," which was published under a pen name, Paulhan paints an unsentimental picture of the dangers he and his colleagues faced not simply as Résistants but as writers and editors engaged in clandestine publishing. In an episode that has been much recounted, Paulhan, hoping to avoid arrest by the Gestapo and charges of treason, had at one point to dismantle a printing press that he and his colleagues had kept and used in his home and drop it piece by piece into the Seine. Two of his less fortunate colleagues in this operation were subsequently executed.[9]

But what is most astonishing about Paulhan's wartime writings, as distinct from his editorial activities, is only obliquely related to such feats of courage. Their daring and, we believe, the lessons they hold for us today have less to do with their bold expression of either polemical or pacifist positions than with their challenges to conventional wisdom, as we have already suggested—challenges, above all, to received notions of what politics is and where it may, or may not, take place. Thus we learn, in the "Letter on Peace" (1949), that courage can itself be rather treacherous, above all in the context of arguments for war, or against it—not because it is not reliable, or liable to produce and reproduce certain events, but, on the contrary, because men "want to prove their courage every day." The more horrible the descriptions of war on which you base your arguments for peace, explains Paulhan, "the more you offer them the chance they've been dreaming of." In this same text, we learn that the desire for peace does not make us feel righteous but, more often than not, slightly embarrassed:

> It is true that I desire peace, as does everyone else. But I desire it timidly, and, if I can say so, secretly. When I hear the brave M. Philip state that this peace is a question of life or death for us, or the excellent M. Spaak during a fine declamation: "We want peace, and we will not let ourselves

> be attacked by anyone!" or else the delightful Paul Eluard: "We are fighting against war," I am embarrassed. They are right, of course. Yet it seems to me that peace is driven off by battles, by questions of life and death, by fine declamations, who knows, perhaps even by speeches. . . .

Hence the stumbling block, explains Paulhan, of so many "Treatises on Perpetual Peace": "If you desire peace, begin by waging war." The point is not just that all these fine declamations about peace are ridiculous, but that any statement about the lengths to which we will go for peace is bound to drive it off. The problem is not "simply" rhetorical, although it is, in its first and tentative formulations, indistinguishable from what Paulhan analyzes in the name of rhetoric elsewhere.

One way to grasp the place of questions of language or of rhetoric in Paulhan's political writings is therefore simply to emphasize that if, for Paulhan, thoughts are always made of language, this holds equally whether we are thinking about peace, democracy, Europe, Africa, or Asia—or the ingenuity of the foreigner who invents the word "spoon with holes" because he does not know the word "fork" ("Jacob Cow"). In terms of the linguistic and intellectual operations at work here, on a first and enduring level of analysis, there is no difference between the ingenuity of this foreigner, at whom it can seem that we are laughing, and the stupidity of politicians. Hence we are not laughing when we read: "I think we should rank bad reasoning—generated every day by the anxiety to put an end to wars—at the top of the list of horrors of wars." This foreigner makes numerous appearances throughout the texts collected here, regardless of their explicit topic. This emphasis on our relation to the foreigner—to his language or, stranger still, to the passage of his language into our "own"—is in itself enough to illustrate the extent to which, for Paulhan, it can seem that language, if not itself always political, has political dimensions and effects. Hence the early text on the Malagasy proverb is an engagement, not simply with the foreignness of languages, but with questions of force.

But more even than these connections—between foreign policy and foreign language—what drives home the essential linkage of language and politics, power and rhetoric, is, in the end, something even subtler in Paulhan's texts. It is their engagement with the slightest nuance of language, the least little residue of what ought almost not to be there. Hence, in "Democracy Calls on the First to Come Along," we can make out, even if only barely, the outlines of the proper subject of democracy, and yet we cannot find him anywhere. In "The Bee," conversely, we find concentrated in this "almost nothing" or "trifle" (*peu de chose*), which seems to make almost no difference, the very figure of resistance. The bee sting, for all its seeming ordinariness, requires of us, if we follow Paulhan, the deepest of commitments—like the opacities and resistances of his own language. Whether they deal with such explicitly political questions as democracy and occupation, the Munich Pact and Vichy, or with the flowers of rhetoric, all of the texts selected for this volume give us the chance, we believe, to explore the seeming insignificance of such contretemps, of the rhyme without reason and, in so doing, to renew our own commitments.

Translations were made from the versions of Paulhan's texts appearing in the *Œuvres complètes*, v. 1–5 (Paris: Cercle du Livre Précieux, 1966–70).[10] We have reproduced the marginal notes appearing in this edition as well as the introductory blurbs accompanying many of the texts, which were written by Paulhan in the course of preparing the texts for reedition. This labor was interrupted in 1968, when he died.

We gratefully acknowledge the suggestions that were made by the readers of the manuscript for the University of Illinois Press. We are also indebted to Michael Syrotinski for his willingness to advise on selections and other decisions at the project's early stages and for his invitation to publish earlier versions of two of the translations collected here, "The Bee" and "Democracy Calls on the First to Come Along," in a special issue of *Yale French Studies* (no. 106) on Paulhan. Above all, we would like to thank Willis Regier for his own inimitable editorial vision and unflagging support of this project.

Notes

1. In English, this is thanks to the recent efforts of a handful of scholars. See, in particular, Michael Syrotinski, *Defying Gravity: Jean Paulhan's Interventions in Twentieth-Century French Intellectual History* (Albany: State University of New York, 1998); Martyn Cornick, *Intellectuals in History: The Nouvelle Revue Française under Jean Paulhan, 1925–1940* (Amsterdam and Atlanta: Rodopi, 1995); Michael Syrotinski, ed., *The Power of Rhetoric, the Rhetoric of Power: Jean Paulhan's Fiction, Criticism, and Editorial Activity, Yale French Studies* 106 (2004); and, most recently, Anna-Louise Milne, *The Extreme In-Between: Jean Paulhan's Place in the Twentieth Century* (Oxford: Legenda, 2006).

2. Michael Syrotinski, "Editor's Preface," *Yale French Studies* 106 (2004): 2.

3. It seems safe to say that Paulhan's emphasis on rhetoric and on literary language accounts for his influence on deconstruction and contemporary literary theory, as witnessed by the echoes and, in some instances, direct citations we find of his work in texts by Paul de Man and Jacques Derrida. For a thoroughgoing account of the controversies that have been sparked by claims for Paulhan's relationship to deconstruction, see Syrotinski, *Defying Gravity*, 1–23. This influence has also been established, more circuitously, through Paulhan's exchange with Maurice Blanchot (another "secret" source of contemporary theory). For Blanchot's first and most important essay on Paulhan, see "*Comment la littérature est-elle possible?*" a review essay of *Les Fleurs de Tarbes* first published in the *Journal des Débats* in November 1941; reprinted in book form in Blanchot, *Faux Pas* (Paris: Gallimard, 1943), 97–107; in English as *Faux Pas*, trans. Charlotte Mandell (Stanford, Calif.: Stanford University Press, 2001), 76–84.

4. Although published in 1970, *Le Repas et l'amour chez les Mérinas* is typically dated 1912–13. A single chapter of Paulhan's dissertation has appeared in *Les Cahiers Jean Paulhan* 2 (Paris: Gallimard, 1982): 266–311.

5. Jean Paulhan, "*Les Hain-Tenys (sic), Poésie de dispute,*" *Œuvres complètes* (Paris: Cercle du Livre Précieux I, 1966): 70 (our translation).

6. *The Flowers of Tarbes, or, Terror in Literature,* trans. Michael Syrotinski (Urbana and Chicago: University of Illinois Press, 2006), 34.

7. As he indicates in a letter to Artaud in *Choix de lettres II. Traité des jours sombres* (Paris: Gallimard, 1992), 215.

8. From this date forward, Paulhan committed himself to the Resistance and focused his energies on the underground journal *Lettres françaises,* which he cofounded. The *NRF* resumed publication from December 1940 to June 1943 under the directorship of collaborator Drieu La Rochelle. Paulhan's relationship to the journal during the German occupation nonetheless remained complex, and he kept a close, worried eye on it. Indeed, the table of contents of each issue was systematically shown to him before going to press.

9. For a thoroughgoing account of Paulhan's wartime activity, see Richard Rand's introduction to Jean Paulhan, *Of Chaff and Wheat: Writers, War, and Treason* (Urbana and Chicago: University of Illinois Press, 2004).

10. A new edition of Paulhan's works is in preparation at Gallimard but only the first volume, consisting of the collected fiction, has been published at the time of going to press.

I

On Poetry and Proverbs

THE EXPERIENCE OF THE PROVERB

At the beginning of his career, Paulhan spent three years in Madagascar (1908–10), which was then a French colony, where he taught as a *professeur de lettres* at a secondary school in Tananarive. His subjects included Latin, philosophy, and French literature and language. During his stay, he undertook a serious study of the *hain-teny*, a kind of proverb peculiar to the Merina people, and upon returning to France published an anthology of more than 150 of these proverbs he had collected, classified, and translated, under the title *Les Hain-Teny Mérinas. Poésies populaires malgaches* (The Merina Hain-Teny: Popular Malagasy Poetry) (Paris: Librairie Paul Geuthner, 1913). In this same period, Paulhan began work on a doctoral dissertation at the Sorbonne, "The Semantics of the Proverb." This project, however, was never completed. Paulhan corresponded with noted French sociologist and anthropologist Lucien Lévy-Bruhl, who was to direct the dissertation, about the possibility of moving forward with a *soutenance de thèse* as late as 1936—more than twenty-six years after Paulhan first approached him with the project, as Lévy-Bruhl rather wryly points out in his letter.

The essay was first published in 1925, in the journal *Commerce* (no. 5). In it, Paulhan recounts the difficulties he encountered as he studied and tried (and failed) to understand the meaning of the *hain-teny* and nevertheless eventually learned to make use of them effectively. This same "experience" also became the subject of a lecture, entitled "*Le Langage sacré*" (Sacred Language), that Paulhan gave in Paris in May 1939 at the College of Sociology, founded shortly before by Georges Bataille, Roger Caillois, and Michel Leiris. The essay is included in the *Œuvres complètes*, volume 2, pp. 99–124.

THE EXPERIENCE OF THE PROVERB

Translated by Eric Trudel

(I spent many years in Madagascar, living from the very beginning with a Malagasy family whose chores I made every effort to share, and, more than the chores, their thoughts and worries. This did not happen without some gaffes.

I will not consider here whether the particular difficulties I encountered in proverbs are specific to Malagasy, or common to all languages. I wish only to describe, as carefully as possible, my experience and the discoveries—or the ruses—that helped me to overcome these difficulties.)

1.

Before I applied myself to acquire knowledge of proverbial language, I felt its existence in a very vivid manner because of the discomfort and, if I may say so, the harm it caused me.

I learned Malagasy directly, as I used it, and did not allow myself to read or write during the first year. Though I already knew how to use most of the sentences that repeatedly came up in everyday conversations, I began to suspect that my language differed from the Madagascans': the breadth of my vocabulary was not at issue, nor was the correctness of my syntax—strangely, it is only much later that such worries came to me, when I should have reasonably ceased to have them—but it seemed as if my words were not worthy and lacked a certain weight, some value, or a tone of conviction. They appeared deprived of the very part of themselves that would have forced my listeners to accept them. I had no choice but to acknowledge, whenever I wished to engage in any discussion, that I perhaps knew how to express my thoughts, but not how to impose them. It is not uncommon to see, in any meeting where all members have an equal right to speak, wise and wisely presented opinions fail to "stick" and fade away without leaving any trace. It is not enough to say that no one listens to them; it is as if no one had even heard them. This failure can be attributed to some flaw on the speaker's part, to his timidity, for instance. According to a Malagasy saying, an orphan, even if he makes some pertinent point, will not be understood: because he has never had the confidence provided by parental love.

Although I recognized in my own speech a flaw that was similar in its effects, I did not attribute it to something in me, and refused to see in it a character trait. I had every reason to suppose, on the contrary, that the authority I felt was lacking was exterior in nature, material, and that it was simply because of my ignorance that I was not in possession of it: as if there were, hidden inside common language, and momentarily peeking through its surface, a second, esoteric language, and that any influence, by tacit agreement, was owed to its use. There exist, in any language, secondary or specialized ways of speaking, such as the slang of a trade association, in spoken French, or literary language. The brutal intrusion of either one into a conversation can be surprising, touching, or unpleasant. At first, I looked upon this second Malagasy language, when I was able to perceive it, in much the same way: some sort of disproportion of its words, its structure, its accent, when compared with the sentences that had preceded it, often made me laugh. But this feeling of irony was, each time, cut short by the fact that I could see that this second language was held in high esteem. It was greeted with a consideration that no other sentences were shown. In the end, I had to accept that this language corresponded to a particular degree or mode of thought and expression, or that it caused this new mode to appear by its presence alone.

I quickly learned to identify this language each time for sure, and to isolate it. Sometimes it would come and disrupt the tone of a discussion that had gone on too long, would rush it along and force it to its conclusion; or else it would nip a nascent squabble in the bud. This was how every dispute in the Hova family, with whom I lived, ended: what was needed was a proverb—and really a proverb was enough—to bring it to an end. I came to the conclusion that their discussions were nothing more than a way of waiting for this proverb: I would think to myself and bet, based on the turn of the conversation, on the time it would take for it to emerge. I could sometimes sense it was approaching, as the discussion was hurrying up and becoming more straitened—just as one feels that the refrain of a song is coming.

The proverb was also similar to a refrain—or to some refrains, in any case—because of its obscurity, its bad timing. I would occasionally recognize it by the strangeness of the words it contained that were new in the conversation and different from what had until then been the topic. I had other signs of its presence: it was spoken rather quickly, and sketched more than said—but with remarkable dignity and seriousness. Rabe would go so far as to stand up each time he uttered a proverb; Ralay would stretch out his arms and lean forward. Whenever Rasoa began speaking in proverbs, I felt that she was about to tell us some grave piece of news, unrelated to our conversation: an accident, a death. I never saw anyone interrupt a proverb. On the contrary, it was as if everyone were giving it his or her full attention as if to further it, to ease its progress—as when one supports with "all one's heart" an acrobat during a dangerous stunt; or when, as they join in the refrain of an operetta, those who were opponents a moment ago all of a sudden find themselves in harmony.

I was not yet trying, however, to grasp the meaning of these obscure words but was already keenly aware of the attention and the cooperation that were required all around me. As soon as these words had been uttered, I would have the impression that the previous conversation had, in a way, led to them, as if it had raised itself to their level. My own language, because it was deprived of them, seemed completely monotonous to me.

I am only describing an impression as carefully as possible, at the risk of its seeming naive. In conversations in which a prayer, a command, an insult—or some other form of language that indicates or brings about a temporary or more lasting difference of dignity between interlocutors—did not intervene, proverbial language seemed to me to play the role of this command or this insult, depending upon the circumstances, or even of the insistence conveyed by a single sentence repeated over and over. It played the same role, if you will, without going to such lengths and without needing to leave language behind.

It was not long before I encountered more precise reasons for being surprised. I have said that I could find no reasons external to language that could have accounted for the proverb's influence: I had no choice but to make do with the proverb's meaning. But my first attempts to fathom this meaning met with unexpected difficulties.

RAJAONA: Let's take a filanjana to the market.[1]

ME: —It's only an hour away, let's go on foot instead. The filanjana is for the elderly.

RAJAONA: —Respect is bought. If you walk to the market, people will laugh at you.

Respect is bought is a proverb. I fail to notice it, and besides, none of the words has warned me it is coming. Considering it nothing more than the continuation of the previous sentence, I reply:

—I would rather do as I please, and get a little less respect. Besides, you can be sure that . . .

However, it does not take me long to notice that I am speaking in vain, and that no one is listening. I stop; the discussion fails to get going again. Rajaona, obviously, is unscathed. But Rabe, who was listening, replies for me:

—And here is what I have to say: you are struck by the proverb *the cicada's voice is heard above the fields, but its body can be held in one hand.* You are not rich, you should not be so proud.

As if he had been waiting only for this, Rajaona answers in turn with a new proverb. My objection was no more taken into account than if it had been uttered in an unknown language.

I have to explain this failure, and other failures I experienced of the same order, by supposing that the meaning was not exactly where I thought it was. My response stemmed from a sentence that ran more or less thus: respect needs to be bought (and how else could one obtain it, if not by some sacrifice; besides, are we not all eager to acquire it? . . .). But I realize now that such a detailed reflection is completely unrelated to the actual sentence that Rajaona spoke: the meaning of each of these words must be less present than I imagined, because Rajaona does not recognize them in my answer. Adventures like these have led me to believe in the existence of a special language, one that will not tolerate any intrusion of everyday language. At the same time, it seems to me that, having reached this height, the discussion cannot subsequently wane.

Rainipatsa says to his son Ralay:

But you need to decide on taking a wife. You are of marriageable age.

To which Ralay responds:

—Hey! Father, I don't want people to say: *no sooner has he got himself a wife than he runs for divorce.*

Here I venture a remark along the lines of, "The fact that you marry hastily does not imply that you will want to seek divorce just as quickly; one can happen without the other. . . ." Nobody hears me. Rainipatsa, defeated on these grounds, transfers his grievances elsewhere. But there is more. Rainipatsa was under the impression, as I realize later on, that I shared Ralay's view. This is when, in the course of transferring his grievances to another topic, he answers:

—No matter what you say, both of you, Ralay is my only child; I am counting on him to carry on our lineage. . . .

Later on, however, as I repeat my remark to Rainipatsa, he finally understands it, merely quotes the proverb again, and thinks he can thus convince me of my mistake:

—But since *no-sooner-has-he-got-himself-a-wife-than-he-runs-for-divorce!*

Thus I have to imagine that the connections internal to the proverb do not remain what they seem. Ralay did not mean to say that one decision made in haste was likely to lead to another: rather, he mentioned a fact that included both of them at once, without any possibility of their being distinguished. It was as if he had said: "And what do you make of the *haste-to-marry-and-to-get-a-divorce-immediately?* Does this not cross your mind?" A comparison can help to clarify things:

CEDES: It's okay for this once, but don't try to revisit it. A word to the wise is enough!

Let us imagine the following reply:

MIRE: —It's not always the case that, because one sees a danger coming, one knows how to avoid it . . .

or any other similar thought. At first, it will seem to hew too faithfully to the apparent crux of the proverb, absurd, unrelated to the conversation. This proverb did not in any way exclude the possibility of a word's not being enough to the wise. There was no question of this; the only acceptable equivalent, perhaps, of the proverb's meaning would be: "Watch out!" or "You've been warned," just as the equivalent of the proverb on haste would be: "Calm down. Let's not do anything too fast!" But then it is the proverb's influence that becomes unexpected and mysterious.

Things would not improve much when a proverb warned me in advance that it was no ordinary sentence, thanks to the gap between its object and that of the neighboring sentences—this was the most common case—and that it required a particular effort. The confusion of which I spoke before had no more reason for being there; all of my efforts to grasp the proverb would fail nonetheless:

RAINIPATSA: I'm counting on you to carry on our lineage; look at Rainibe, who has already given two granddaughters to his parents.

RALAY: Rainibe has a job and is earning a living. I am not. Do you not know that *one who dances without drums is laughed at?*

The proverb suggests that money is no less necessary to a married couple than the beat of a drum to dancers. This, at least, is clear. It would be sufficient for me, in order to use this proverbial language when needed, simply to remember it. For a few weeks, I think it appropriate to speak of drums in connection with money, or of a cicada in connection with vanity: with no success. I resort to the most unexpected metaphors: to the Madagascans—and, to be honest, to myself—it seems that I am only playing a game, whose significance furthermore escapes them.

But there is more: the Madagascan who utters a proverb often seems unaware that he is using an image. One needs only to reflect the image back to him to catch him off guard.

RABE: How do you expect me to defend myself against these people? *The dead ox doesn't protect himself from flies.*

I answer:

But you are still a very lively ox, and robust.

To this, Rahaja kindly replies, as if pointing out an error of taste:

How can you call Rabe an ox?

Because of these various failures, I was prevented from recognizing any of the proverb's features other than its mysterious authority, linked to the absence of multiple meanings and possibilities for meaning the proverb seemed at first glance to imply. In the end, these two features being in my mind more tightly linked to one another, I came very close to believing that the proverb owed its power to this obscurity alone.

2.

The reader may find, based on what I have just recounted, that I was clumsier than most. And I have no doubt that a French peasant would have fared much better in my position. But I was not aware, before coming to Madagascar, of the existence or even the possibility of proverbial language. Or rather, I had a few abstract and literary notions of its existence—notions more liable to mislead me than to set me on the right path. No doubt this clumsiness also explains why I was so eager to be surprised by the proverbs I was faced with, and why I eventually gained a knowledge of them different from the peasant's.

Trying to explain the cause of my confusion to my Malagasy friends presented a particularly disconcerting difficulty. Their answers, though given willingly, were marked by a clumsiness matching my own. As soon as I wanted to focus their attention on the proverb, naked, isolated from the sentence or the speech that contained it, they would get flustered, dodge my question, and seem deliberately to avoid grasping—in order to then explain it to me—an object of which they no doubt had a perfectly clear idea.

Thus, if I ask what this proverb means: *a lark's egg on the side of the road; I am not the guilty one, 'tis the lark.*

> RALAY: But where did you hear it? What was the discussion about?
>
> —I don't remember. Just tell me what the proverb means.

Ralay thinks for a moment and then answers:

> Imagine you are a raffia merchant. You go to the market; your first client is a peasant who does not know what things are worth. He gives you the price you ask for, even if it is ten piasters. And your

> neighbor tells you: "This is wrong, you are cheating the poor man." Then you say: "You must be kidding. It is his own stupidity that cheated him. *A lark's egg on the side of the road; I am not the guilty one, 'tis the lark.*"

I manage in this way to grasp the meaning of the proverb: it is about a passerby who sees the egg, takes it with him, and tells himself: "I have nothing to be ashamed of, the lark should have hidden it better." Why was I not immediately given this simple explanation? I suggest it, but nobody is interested. Is it accurate or not? Scarcely a peep. "There's nothing wrong with it," observes Rajaona as I insist, "but that's not exactly it." It seems that my explanation is at once indisputable and pointless.

> IBOALA: This time, I think you will have learned your lesson. Fifty francs lost in one evening!
>
> BELALAO: Ah! Now is when I must gamble, to win them back.
>
> IBOALA: Beware. The proverb says: *what is hoped for is not caught, what is lost was once held.*
>
> BELALAO: That is not the issue here. If one is patient, the moment always comes when *the calf is born in autumn; joy and wealth at once.*

The discussion goes on. A bit later, I question Iboala about the meaning of the proverb: *what is hoped for...* "When did I say it?" he immediately asks. I remind him. He explains: "Oh! It is often the case that gamblers persist, no matter what you tell them...." Thus, in order to give meaning to the proverb, he must situate it first, surround it by the same words that were set into motion by the discussion. He refuses to imagine it outside of these connections. If I insist, he seems to see in my insistence the sign of some hostility: am I going to think that he is wrong, am I going to be the one teaching him how to speak properly? It seems that there is some difficulty within the proverb, some core that, before it can be assimilated, requires that one must first consider the proverb as it is used, as it comes into play. It does not stand on its own.

I am now better able to describe the feature common to all the answers I was given. These answers all seemed to assume that I already knew the proverb, or more exactly whatever it was the proverb was about, and that my uncertainty had to do only with the way this thing was expressed.

When someone would quote this expression to me—and all the more so as it was familiar to me—it was with the feeling of catching me out, as if a lack of goodwill alone had led me to seek clarification.

RAZAY: You ought not, Rasoa, to wear your new lamba to go to the market. If there is a crush, you'll come back in rags.
RASOA: Not to worry, I'll stay out of harm's way.
ME: We always think that we'll be able to run away and then, caught in the fray, it's not so easy to escape.
RAZAY: Maybe Rasoa thinks that she is *the bull of clay that will not lose its horns.*[2]

Once Rasoa is gone I ask Razay the meaning of *bull-of-clay.* . . . "But it is this: we always think that we'll be able to run away . . ." and repeats my entire sentence, as if satisfied, but also avenged, having caught me in the act of feigning ignorance.

Here I must thank for their assistance the young Madagascans educated in the European way, free—or claiming to be free—of any allegiance to these proverbs, and who, considering them to be mere sentences (stupid sentences, they would add, and almost meaningless), greatly helped me to make sense of them. In fact, I did not trust these young people whose language contained, alongside pure Malagasy words, too many English or French ones, barely modified. (Sometimes they even treated these foreign words with the same respect their parents showed for proverbs, which scandalized me.)

To be sure, they did not spontaneously grasp the proverbs' meanings: they would sometimes resort to etymology, or would quote some ancestors' dictate in which a proverb figured, but above all they would remind me of the various connections and images I had had to let go; their meaning was cobbled together. It did not matter: this attitude of indifference was providing me with the share of inaccuracy I needed. A difference of opinion, a nuance, would put these young Madagascans in the same predicament as I myself was owing to my ignorance. I could not hold too great a grudge against the elders of whom I had initially inquired, and who had reacted to my ignorance as if it had been caused by a difference of opinion.

It did not take long for me to realize that the problem I faced was, perhaps, even more complex than I had imagined. To be exact, it did not seem to be only my problem (I could no longer hope, from that point forward, to consider my ignorance of the language the sole explanation), but also the Madagascans', and a problem even for those who, in my eyes, were the most gifted speakers. Thus it could easily happen that a proverb, far from meeting with a general agreement and approval, would abruptly change course and, as it were, fall flat. In such cases, it was not thought appropriate to answer anything apart from: "But this is not what it's about. . . . What did you mean? . . ." Or else this, which would confuse me even more: "Words, nothing but words . . . what are you telling us? . . . Enough with your proverbs!" (the very thing that I wanted to reply to a proverb when it was used against me). And they would say nothing more. In the end, everything would happen as if a proverb, when used incorrectly and forced to reveal its proverbial nature, came to the aid of the opinion it was meant to attack rather than to the one it was meant to support. Its author would have no choice but to immediately invent some excuse, some other proverb. It was not easy for him to erase the ridicule of his initial blunder.

Thus it seemed to me that a proverb could never be used without some element of risk. I compared it to a difficult exercise, one that we cannot ever perform entirely without thinking. But I write this last observation down only in order to be as thorough as I can, and to add to my initial surprises a new surprise that seemed, at first, to contradict them. I learned very little from it. It did not increase my knowledge. When I wanted to remember, in the early days, some example of a failed use of proverbs, I could do so only with great difficulty (whereas the successes stayed fixed in my memory). It was as if nothing at all had happened: there was not one word, one turn of phrase that could be said to contribute to the failure more than another. Memory and reflection had no hold over these examples, characterized as they were by an absence of success alone. It is also possible that I did not make much effort to remember them; determined as I was to make progress, I was doubtless trying to keep my mind free of what seemed like examples not to follow. I could have concluded, based on this experience, that there was little reason to be discouraged by a clumsiness that I shared with the Madagascans. But I chose rather to believe that the difficulties that lay ahead were enormous.

3.

A few months go by. My language is in its turn starting to contain proverbs. Of course, more often than not I quote them innocently in some story or another, "just for the heck of it," and yet I manage now and then to bring them into a discussion where they support my cause.

How was I able to acquire this rudimentary knowledge? It is not because I discovered, one day, in a flash of meaning, the cause of the difficulties and contradictions described earlier. No, the progress was made unwittingly and in an obscure way. Certainly the illusions and the mistakes we have seen were useful to me at first. The discovery of an image, the analysis of a meaning—although these things prevented me from giving myself over to the free play of proverbs, they at least provided me with a framework and categories by which to classify and later retrieve these proverbs from memory. Their help was insufficient, I will readily admit, and even dangerous, because the proverb is at once more and less than an argument or a metaphor. It is both of these in a fixed form. It requires, in order to remain a proverb, that the very same words composing it be called back in an identical order.

I am exaggerating on purpose. In actual fact, many proverbs can be modified slightly, shortened or expanded without losing their proverbial quality. But this kind of alteration requires a tact and a flexibility I was not even close to possessing. In my view the slightest modification was enough to cast the proverb back into common language—and such was, in reality, the effect of the alterations I myself devised. Thus *one who dances without drums is laughed at* was a proverb; but such sentences as, "Who has ever danced without drums?" or "Here's something laughable: he is dancing without a drum" were no longer proverbs. Remembering only the image was bound to mislead me. I had to recall the entire proverbial sentence, as if it had been a single word.

At this stage, I did not encounter the difficulties that might have been expected. I had been prepared by the failure of my first interpretive attempts, which had led me to think that proverbs were absurd and almost totally meaningless, to consider each proverb as a whole, a single block that I needed to grasp in its entirety, all at once. At the same time, I had been learning Malagasy, until that point, by sentences more than by words: the work required of me here was not any different. It just so happened that the sets of arbitrary words I wanted to remember came with certain particular rules of composition, certain laws of meaning. Thus any proverb could become a mold, a stencil likely to provide me, given a few alterations, with hundreds of reproductions. I easily went from:

Soul of the slave: to destroy.

to:

Soul of Iketaka[3]*: to play hard to get.*
Soul of a child: to think about nothing.

In the same vein:

If the teeth are broken, the head is to blame.

became:

If the hair is white, the head is to blame.

Or still:

How a blind man protects himself: when he's been touched, he leans aside.

gave rise to:

How a mouse dodges blows: when it's been touched, it jumps aside.

Subsequently, the abstract framework common to an entire family of proverbs would come to mind first and be filled with words only afterward.

But I am making too much of a schoolboy's trick. Nor was this trick alone enough to do the job: I would frequently remember some sentence that I knew was a proverb, but without having a better sense of its meaning. I decided to remember, for each sentence of this kind, an abstract word that would give me an equivalent. Thus: *if the eye is blinded, the head is to blame* would be linked to the idea of *solidarity;* and *how a blind man protects himself . . .* linked to *being slow off the mark.* For *its voice is heard above the fields, but its body can be held in one hand,* I thought of *vanity.*

This was not a very reliable method. It was valid only for a few proverbs, and it was foolproof for none. It is enough that these associations had been useful to me: they would eventually fade away on their own when I managed to make a proverb my own, and the associations could even reappear later on if some aspect of this proverb's meaning still eluded me.

Help came to me in the course of this study mainly from other quarters than those I had anticipated. I have suggested that all that was Malagasy, be it mores, or traits of character or of spirit, would throw me into a mild enthusiasm. I endeavored to share this enthusiasm with my friends. In a letter I sent to one of them I offered, as proof of my savages' ingenuity and gift for observation, a long list of proverbs. After all, I was doing what most travelers do—but perhaps it was more surprising coming from me, for whom these proverbs were necessarily anything but a clever observation. Affection has ingenious ways.

In any case I myself am fooled by this affection—perhaps I was forming, to myself, an image of these proverbs completely different from the one finally imposed by my own experiences. After I have quoted some fifty proverbs such as these:

Little girl watching the games: it is when she is leaving that she is noticed.[4]

or:

The house is swept only once the wagging tongue is gone.[5]

I admire how shrewd and telling are these observations. Each seems to shed light on an order of things that until now had remained obscure to me. I am led to read the collections of Malagasy proverbs I can come by, not as one would read a dictionary, but rather as a succession of little dramas or fables, each including its complete meaning:

Let a blind man guide you, and you'll end up in a ditch.

Or else as a collection of maxims:

Men are riches.

Not that all proverbs lend themselves to such interpretation. I am especially interested in those that offer some hint of paradox or malice; the proverbs that are simply obvious appear to me, on the contrary, rather useless, and I ignore them. It is enough for me to encounter thirty proverbs out of a hundred capable of intriguing me or teaching me something to suppose that these are the "true" proverbs. As for the others, I must not be understanding them entirely, or else they are second-rate proverbs of little consequence. I thus arrive at the image of a "Malagasy soul," which is moralistic, shrewd, and critical.

It is worth noting that the evolution of this image went hand in hand with the effective progress I was making in my own use of proverbs. Every day I would add a new nuance to the Malagasy soul that I imagined, and every day a few new proverbs would find their way into my sentences. In the end, however, one fact struck me: they were not the same proverbs in each of these cases. It would happen that I found myself incapable of using a proverb in a discussion because I was pondering its ingenuity and its vividness, as if my thought and my language were unfolding on two different planes. Conversely, proverbs seemingly devoid of any interest, such as:

A piece of stone is stone.

Tears fall when the heart is heavy.

I used these quite easily. This all happened as if there in fact existed an antinomy between the meaning of a proverb and the use to which it was put.

I readily admit that, in this form, the antinomy was accidental. It is likely that, had I decided, on the contrary, to insist on the Malagasy's wisdom, wit, or on their loyalty to the obvious, the paradoxical proverbs would have then entered into my language too effortlessly, so to speak, for me to have had time to notice. Thus I started using these paradoxical proverbs just as successfully as the others, as soon as I stopped considering them as admirable discoveries. On the day I noticed, for example, that the proverb, *The house is swept only once the wagging tongue is gone,* was telling me nothing I could not have learned from the French proverb, *The door of the stable is closed only once the horse has gone;* and that this other, *Let a blind man guide you, and you'll end up in a ditch* could very likely have been imported by a missionary, I treated them both more familiarly, and started to use them as "ready-made sentences." Suddenly, I found myself not having to think about them.

It may seem, in fact, that the first operations, which I discussed earlier, thanks to which I was able to start grasping proverbs, produced precisely the same familiarity, and allowed the same lack of reflection. They divided the proverb into two separate parts, one composed of matter, the proverb's words and sentence, and the other composed of the abstract idea attached, like a tag, to this lifeless sentence, and without any internal link, such that it was never necessary to reconstruct this proverb's precise meaning in order to use it. I could use it, it seemed, only on condition of this division.

There is little doubt that it was also the effect and the outward repercussions of such an antinomy I had remarked in the first place—either when my attempts to grasp a proverb based on its apparent meaning had failed, or when the Madagascans had been unable to answer my query and retrieve the proverb's meaning from its usage in order to explain it. Thus my advances with regard to proverbial language seemed to consist less in resolving than in prolonging, within me, the very differences and oppositions that had puzzled me from the start.

4.

Another year or so goes by. My language is now, I believe, as rich in proverbs as a Madagascan's. And yet, I have made very little progress in solving the difficulty that has preoccupied me to this point. It seems, rather, that I have lost the initial interest and curiosity that bound me to it. If I try to recall and clarify the thoughts seemingly forced upon me at first by these proverbs, they now appear importunate. If I did not try to maintain them, they would undoubtedly fall to pieces and vanish. But there is more. My new thoughts about these proverbs are hardly more satisfying, nor any easier to remember.

It is true that I no longer have the feeling that my language is monotonous, lacking gravity and conviction. And I no longer imagine that Madagascans share some secret understanding that eludes me. These are, of course, only negative characteristics, but it is not unusual for me now to "cut short" a discussion that is dragging on with a proverb, and to notice a certain disproportion of tone and accent between my proverb and the sentences that precede or follow it, as if my words had been made, with its arrival, hasty and more pressing. I can also feel that the agreement thus established by this proverb between my interlocutor and myself is more intimate and firm, and that my interlocutor becomes in a way more familiar to me. If I choose to call this familiarity or this agreement an "influence," it is then easy to think that I owe to the proverb my new confidence and the fact of having been able to show myself fully and openly convinced. Finally, it is possible, if need be, for me to repeat every one of my initial observations, but this time as if from within.

If need be. There is, in fact, a common feature of these observations that immediately gives me pause: there is not one among them that does not seem to me in some way inexact and out of place as soon as I endeavor to express it. In the case, for example, of my confidence, I find it difficult to imagine that it—or my success—can be owed to my usage of the proverb. It would seem, rather, that it stems precisely from the truth of my words. Thus I gladly withdraw behind these successful words,

I take my leave, I almost ask to be forgiven for being so right; I would willingly suggest that it is not my fault, that this is just the way things are. In the end, if the question must absolutely by tackled from this angle, it will likely seem to me that it is thanks to my confidence that I have said the proverb, and not the proverb that gave me the confidence; and I will believe that, far from having attempted to influence my interlocutor with the proverb, it is the proverb that has influenced me. But this is asking too much of feelings that vanish upon taking shape.

If I consider, on the other hand, the difference of tone between the proverb and common sentences, I will no doubt observe the following: such a difference takes place in one specific case only, when my proverb fails and not when it succeeds. I am then reminded of it, I ask myself what mistake I made in placing it infelicitously, and I finally appreciate how ridiculous was the solemnity—with which, I realize suddenly, I uttered it. In any other case, it is not enough to say that this disproportion has gone unnoticed: I cannot even imagine it. I would not be happy about owing some measure of my success to the clever use of sentences. Sometimes, when I notice that I have already heard in "proverb form" the words I have just uttered, I feel somewhat embarrassed, as if these words had, because of this, been taken away from me, as if they had nothing to do with me. Thus it is not enough to say that the observations sketched above are in some respect inaccurate. It seems that they may even be dangerous and that the proverb will work only on condition that it is not seen as a proverb. We might even say, to convey such a paradoxical event, that the proverb is, in any case, endowed with a singular importance, but that the worst way to account for this importance is to say that it is due to the proverb. The difficulty, when tackled head-on, can appear insurmountable. The more I press myself and strive to be sincere, the more it seems that *nothing* happens when I utter a proverb: I mean, nothing that belongs to language, nothing that can be expressed by relating it to this singular kind of sentence we call "proverb." The fact that I have lost my initial curiosity with regard to the proverb should no longer be cause for surprise: at the very moment I thought I had reached an explanation for my concern, the very terms by which I understood this concern are taken away from me.

Because any direct observation of the proverb in the moment of its action seems impossible here, it remains to be seen if there might be a way of approaching it indirectly, cunningly, by taking advantage of some mishap of this action. I was to become aware, as I became more familiar with the use of proverbs, that to depict the proverb—as I have done to this point—either as failing definitively or as meeting with unqualified success was to simplify matters too much. Quite to the contrary, it was the intermediary cases that now concerned me most and that I deemed the most "interesting": those cases where the proverb, uttered incorrectly and introduced without much rigor, could still be "recovered," bolstered by an ingenious explanation; or else those cases where, foreseeing some obstacle to the action of the proverb I intended to utter, I made sure to remove it or to circumvent it in advance. It was a matter, in both of these cases, of steadying or rectifying my own effect on the proverb: the only difference being that the proverb was, in the one case, yet to be said and, in the other, already spoken. In the first case, the singular operation that had eluded me so completely a moment ago had already taken place, and the goal was now to maintain it. In the second case, it was necessary to anticipate this operation and set it up in advance. It so happens that I was, in this way, able to detect, on account of one difficulty or the other, markedly different figures of the proverb.

At some point I decide to use proverbs in the discussion I am preparing to have. I try to select these proverbs, as much as possible, in advance. I spoke of confidence a moment ago. I have not yet moved beyond the stage of risk. I have the impression that, in saying the proverb, I am going to court some danger, and that it will "really be something" if it succeeds, but that this success is far from certain. Therefore, I go out of my way to take no chances. I choose my proverbs very carefully: I weigh them up, I assess them. If Rasendra, whose fondness for taverns I am about to criticize, invokes his duty to follow his friends, I will reply with: *Let a blind man guide you, and you'll end up in a ditch.* If he insists on the necessary propriety—to prove he is "up to it," to preserve his rank, to "pay his round"—I will answer: *The cicada's voice is heard above the fields, but its body can be held in one hand.* And, if he objects that he does not want to give the impression that he is poor: *Whoever chats with the wealthy burns his door when he goes home.*[6] I make every effort to ensure that this proverb, when I say it, will not present my interlocutor with insurmountable difficulties of understanding. I do not want the image, although it should be unexpected enough to strike Rasendra, to sound forced or overdone. Its coherence, the sequence of ideas it contains, should take only a slight effort to discover. Finally, because I never stop imagining a possible failure, I try to remember and to summon all the proverbs I know until I have enough to react to the many different cases that may come up, so that I will be able to express these cases as I please and transform to my advantage the very objections Rasendra will raise.

Here we have a first perspective on the proverb—one unlikely, in the end, to surprise us. The proverb is here taken, before it has come into play, for a *sentence* of some authority, suited to expressing this or that given fact, on the condition that nothing in the details of this sentence's meaning will differ from the given fact (as can happen with a word that is at once easy and difficult to introduce because its etymology is too obvious). "This is a matter for *whoever chats with the wealthy* . . ." I might say to myself. Or, "this is precisely what one calls *the voice of the cicada*. . . ." Meaning: these are the words appropriate to this situation, this is the sentence that it calls for. Here, however, it is not all that useful to insist, or to give new examples: there is no other way of thinking about the proverb that could be more common or readily accepted. This way of thinking was at the very root of my early observations, and if I later abandoned it, as will now be obvious, it was only to be brought back to it by my clumsiness. This clumsiness was not unlike that in which I initially found myself because of my ignorance, only this time it was desired, sought after, and stemming from my concern not to be caught off guard by any possible reply.

There is, however, a second point of view from which I can now examine the proverb. I have said that the proverb could seem elusive in the instant it comes into play. Except that, on occasion, this instant can be prolonged. Even more than this, I sometimes find myself accidentally forced to keep it going—and thus forced to shed light on it, to develop it, if only for a moment. This is what happens when, not meeting right away with the strong support I vaguely expected, I go back over my words, start from the beginning again, and try to show that "I was right." I justify myself after the fact, or rather I maintain myself—although perhaps not without artifice and self-consciousness. A slight failure is liable to disclose the features of the enigmatic state that concerns us here. Only this time it is not the failure we were expecting and tried to minimize in advance but rather one that happens after the fact, following the naive use of the proverb, in which there was no time to modify anything, and when the proverb, thrown out there, must work as it is. We might easily catch it as it unfolds.

Let us follow this discussion as it opens:

RASENDRA: How can I just stop going to the café all of a sudden? I cannot abandon all my friends without explanation.

> Me: You can start by drinking a bit less, by spending no more than an hour or two with them. Of course, you have not yet been reduced to having to borrow money, but when you go somewhere, you have no choice but to walk. *Whoever chats with the wealthy burns his door when he goes home.*

Rasendra does not seem to be affected. He does not understand. I insist:

> —This is what I was saying: because you waste your time drinking with friends who have more money than you do, you come home penniless.

Or:

> —After all, being forced to walk would not be so terrible, but you are well aware that your family doesn't have enough to eat.

Or still:

> —Even if one isn't running to the pawn shop, it is a crying shame to leave one's family in need.

And so on.

What has happened? In the same way that, as I was preparing to have this discussion, I chose from among many proverbs the one I thought most suited to express my concerns, I am now stating the facts, I am forming the sentences that seem most capable of explaining the proverb, of making sure it is understood: the sentences that seem most capable—in a word—of expressing it. With this in mind, I keep revising my sentences, fleshing them out, transforming them, making every effort to ensure that Rasendra will not be confused by them. I stick as close as possible to the proverb: thus, to convey the *burning one's door* that it offers me, I move from "having to walk" to the "family that goes hungry," and then to the "crying shame."

Later:

RASENDRA: Don't go getting these ideas just because you saw me drunk two or three days running. First of all, a mere nothing goes straight to my head. Plus it was Ambohibiby's birthday this week; I was obliged to follow my friends.

ME: You really shouldn't let yourself get dragged along. *Let a blind man guide you, and you'll end up in a ditch.*

Seeing that Rasendra is hesitating, I add:

—Did you yourself not say that your friends are dragging you into this and that just a little wine will make you drunk?

I thus express and justify the "blind man who guides you" with "your friends are dragging you into this," and the "ditch" with this immediate drunkenness; moreover, I am justifying them with Rasendra's own words, words he can neither deny nor take back. Thus I discover here in these words, just as, previously, I did in my own words, the same sequence of ideas presented by the proverb. I show that they are perfectly suited to this proverb, that they do not give us any image or any difference that cannot be overcome. The proverb is what unites these words: they seem, at this point, to have no reason for being other than to express the proverb.

This new way of thinking about proverbs is not in the least surprising, any more than was the previous one. It is usually not the *sentence* within the proverb that holds our attention, but on the contrary its subject: a fable, a lesson in morals, a law of nature. The proverbs of any given people have often been seen as the sum of its knowledge and its worldview. If one then wants to explain, in great detail, this worldview and its applications, it is only a matter of language. In the same way, I had initially written down and quoted in my letters those Malagasy proverbs that seemed particularly striking. Thus proverbs are commonly classified not by form but by meaning: proverbs about the family, those about society, about the king. . . .

It seems that the situation I was in earlier has been turned entirely upside down. While I was getting ready to argue, I looked for the best proverb to express the fact (which I took to be a given) that Rasendra ought not drink. The question at that point was, "How will the proverb mean this?" Conversely, as soon as the proverb had been uttered, and given that this proverb represented that fact or, more precisely, *was* that fact, it became a matter of coming up with sentences suited to expressing it accurately and rendering it faithfully. The question had become, "How will these words mean the proverb?" Or better, you could say that the goal was, in both cases, to succeed in expressing a fact with sentences. But a proverb is first a sentence and a fact only subsequently. Conversely, the sentences surrounding it are first facts and then are used as sentences only subsequently.

It is not easy to imagine in detail how such a reversal, whose origin and effects we have just seen, can come about. But irony or humor can give us some approximation of it.

Swift writes:

> Our preacher, neglecting his true topic, which was to show us that theft was an abomination, endeavored to establish in his sermon how little brooks make great rivers, and that every penny counts.[7]

And Claude Tillier:

> It seemed to us afterwards that the orator's only concern was to prove one thing: there are only so many times you can dip an old jug into a well before it breaks.[8] He would stop at nothing to do this.

It could therefore be said that, instead of conveying my opinion through the proverb, I suddenly had to choose to convey the proverb through my opinion. I no longer suppose that it is wrong of Rasendra to drink, and devote myself instead to this new and pressing truth of which Rasendra represents only a particular case: that whoever chats with the wealthy will burn his door when he comes home. I am not able to say the proverb in any fashion unless I immediately believe that "it has happened." It seems that the meaning is not, here, a stable and simple fact that is given together with the proverb, but an invention of this proverb and even some sort of exercise.

As obscure as the distraction and the shift in commitment required by such an exercise remain in themselves, as soon as we accept them, they shed a singular light on the difficulties we encountered upon our initial consideration of the proverb's action. Even their oddities correspond exactly to those that had been holding us back. Thus I had been forced to observe that my confidence seemed to stem, not from my proverb, but from the truth of the events I was referring to. There was a simple reason for this: I could only take this proverb for a true event. As for the disproportions in tone between the proverb and common sentences, I was aware of it only if my proverb failed. But it is also the case that, in the event of its success, it would not have occurred to me to consider this proverb a sentence, and comparable to neighboring sentences. Finally, you have seen how reluctant I was to take these proverbs for what they are—so much so that, in treating of their influence, I did not care to attribute this influence to the "proverb." Language in fact fails us here, and it is difficult to admit that, speaking generally of a *proverb,* we have in mind anything but a given *sentence,* composed of certain words, likely to convey certain facts. We have in mind exactly the opposite of a sentence: an event unhampered by words, a *fact* to be expressed. As soon as we manage to isolate this fact, every difficulty disappears. When I utter the proverb, this is in no way a sentence that I am skillfully introducing: it is a truth whose existence I affirm.

But I must return to my first surprises now. As we have seen, the proverb initially seemed to me to be a sentence, clear or obscure in itself, but at any rate separate from the general flow of conversation. It was a sentence presenting various links, lending itself to certain images such that, in the end, I could not relate it to the topic of the conversation without some effort. At the same time, I had no choice but to recognize that the Madagascans had used the proverb without perceiving theses links or these images. Moreover, it seemed as if the Madagascans, who had failed to understand my proverbs as I was trying to produce them, were only capable of grasping them by means of elaborating them or translating them into common sentences. Thus I had to assume that there was something at the proverb's core requiring that, before it can be grasped, this proverb be considered in the moment of its application, almost in its projection. But we can now say, more simply: in its expression, as if it were a thing, which can be grasped only when we have started to express it. I had mistaken for words what Madagascans understood as things. Such was the source of our misunderstanding.

In much the same vein, what I had later called an antinomy was an analogous misunderstanding, but one I had carried entirely within me. By making a distinction between complex proverbs (those boasting too many unexpected meanings and that were, for this very reason, condemned to remain sentences for me, and to be considered separately from other sentences) and simple, self-evident proverbs (those I had no problem getting into my conversations), I was setting up an opposition similar to the one I was to discover later between a proverb *before* and *after* it is used: one was complex, manifold, difficult to boil down, and the other, on the contrary, natural, self-evident, and demanding only to be expressed quickly, and then applied. A proof of this was that the most complex proverb would easily cross over into the second category if it came to feel natural and familiar to me through repeated encounters. In the end, there is not one among my observations, as contradictory as they may at first have seemed, that cannot find in the following fact its explanation and its place: the operation of the proverb rests entirely on the passage from one of these states to the reverse—or, if you prefer, the passage from one observation to the opposite one. The proverb's success depends on this movement.

If the intention and the general contours of such an exercise are now familiar, there is nonetheless still one feature that remains mysterious: namely, the influence it exerts. Everything happens as if the reversal, or better, the transformation we have witnessed, conferred some merit on its author. Such a transformation is no doubt difficult, and it does not always succeed. But there is more: it also seems so serious and urgent that each of the interlocutors, relinquishing his own opinion for an instant, finds that he has a stake in it. Everything happens as if there were these events—proverbs—that it is laudable or worthwhile to express. We might thus imagine that the success of a difficult expression—without which meaning and our very language are threatened—in some way forces my opponent to acknowledge the confidence and ascendancy I obtain by overcoming this difficulty, because he is just as concerned as I am to see this meaning and this language go on. We would have to say, in this case, that my initial clumsiness had put me on the scent of a more general clumsiness that is, perhaps, inherent to all language. If we tried to name this clumsiness, we would get something like this: certain words must be taken for things. This is not saying enough. These words are, rather, singular things, which it is urgent to *say*, and to say in as exact a way as possible—such that, when it comes to these things, or these words, a whole part of language is used to establish that speaking is possible.

It is possible that my very efforts to penetrate the proverb have misled me, by showing me the proverb in the guise of an effort—and possible that, in the end, in my haste to succeed, I have only taken a detour around the difficulty instead of solving it. My only intention was to describe this difficulty, and these efforts.

JACOB COW THE PIRATE, OR, IF WORDS ARE SIGNS

The integral text of the essay was first published in three successive issues of the journal *Littérature* (nos. 14–16) edited by André Breton, Philippe Soupault, and Louis Aragon in 1920 and is without a doubt the text by Paulhan most closely connected with surrealism. Parts of the text had been published earlier, in *Marges* (no. 60, March 1919) and the *Nouvelle Revue Française* (nos. 78 and 80, March and May 1920). As Pierre Vilar notes in his preface to a recent reedition of the essay, it made enough of a mark to garner the admiration of Paul Nougé and other Belgian surrealists, who paid homage to it in 1924. See *Jacob Cow le pirate* (Paris: Deyrolle Éditeur, 1997), p. 13.

Although rhetoric is, here as elsewhere, the explicit topic of the theories of language advanced, in "Jacob Cow" it is still written with a small "r," and its adversary has not yet been named "Terror," as it will be later. Paulhan's frequent references to esoteric and exotic sources (such as, for example, to Chinese poetry and African languages) and his practice of citing invented authors are much in evidence, anticipating future and increasingly systematic usages of the same idiosyncratic devices. We also see sketched a kind of ethical imperative to accept not simply language's ambiguities, but the undecidable double bind produced by the confrontation, and alternation, between two linguistic worldviews, which will become increasingly urgent in later texts. An earlier English translation of the essay, by Austin Gill, was published in J. L. Hevesi, ed., *Essays on Language and Literature* (Port Washington, N.Y.: Kennikat Press, 1967 [1947].) The original text appears in the *Œuvres complètes,* volume 2, pp. 127–40.

JACOB COW THE PIRATE, OR, IF WORDS ARE SIGNS

Translated by Jennifer Bajorek

FOR PAUL VALÉRY

1. IF WORDS ARE SIGNS, OR, FIVE KILOS OF SUGAR FOR NOTHING

> I became accustomed to asking myself whether words are not the thing in the world least suited to speaking.
>
> Travels of Botzarro, Op. XIII B. 225

It is difficult to talk about words in a detached way, as a painter describes the braying of colors. They are so mixed up with our concern to make use of them that we never make out very clearly where the concern begins and the word leaves off.

Yet there is not an appreciable difference and rift between the word and the sentence, the sentence and the tale. The philosophers observe that we comb our hair and lace our shoes according to the idea we have of the world. The writer, a maker of language, sees and composes himself in imitation of his first opinion about puns.

Hence the gravity of this opinion and the import of any error it contains. One does not reform people who write bad books by repeating to them that they are bunglers. One must help them to come up with two or three sound ideas about language.

IF WORDS ARE SIGNS

We are perfectly ready to suppose that words are for people to express themselves. They are by nature signs of thoughts; as are those junctions or fibers uniting them, down to their slightest variations. The imperfect tense, say the grammar books, expresses. . . .

Such an idea of the sign is not so clear-cut that it can avoid presenting two faces. One is a mistrust of words considered in themselves. For words are not self-sufficient, and it is rather the thought we discover beneath them that is alone the reason they have meaning and its source. Without this thought, they can lead us astray: "Those are," we say, "only words . . . " or "Think before you speak." The other face, however, takes the form of confidence, once thought and word have been rejoined. Then it seems that every word may be illuminated by this thought (none is insuperable: it is difficult to imagine a sentence without any meaning). Or again, conversely, that every thought has its word. "Find the right word," the grammarians advise us, and: "There is nothing that can't be said."

This way of seeing things entails a certain obscurity. It gets tricky explaining that the idea sometimes follows the word, that it comes from it or translates it. Cilia, as she is struggling to explain to the doctor what ails her little girl, discovers her true fear in the course of speaking and is surprised at herself. Atys finally says to Chrysos: "So then, you lied," and each of them reconstructs, on the basis of this word, what he really thought. Here, an idea is the sign of this word, and a way of communicating it, far from the word's being the sign of the idea. Moreover, we know, of this or that poet, that words are his element: he squeezes them, listens to them, waits for them.

FIVE KILOS OF SUGAR FOR NOTHING

Public opinion, like criticism, can get ahead of itself. It is here that we catch hold of words in spontaneous usage, rough and unreserved. I recently read:[1]

FIVE KILOS OF SUGAR

for every reader of
"*L'AVENIR*"

How it works:

A buyer of single issues lays out annually
365 copies at 0,10 F
or 36,50 F

A year's subscription in Paris costs
25 F
and entitles a purchase of 5 kilos of
sugar at 2,20 F per kilo
11 F
or 36 F

Every reader of
"*L'AVENIR*"
can thus obtain, *for nothing*, 5 kilos of sugar.

It is perfectly obvious that the only reader who obtains, roughly, five kilos of sugar for nothing is the buyer of single issues who subscribes, owing to this change. The subscriber can spend eleven francs if he wants sugar. The most faithful buyer of single issues gets nothing.

All three, however, were necessarily intended by the word *reader*. This is how the demonstration works. It gets its value and its proper meaning only on condition of promising a little more than it can deliver.

We will think: "They thought they could con us," and that is that. It would not be a publicity stunt [*réclame*] if each of us could wash his hands of it this easily. Upon a more neutral examination, its ingenuity makes itself felt: namely, that our initial error to a certain extent compromises us and then, as we go further, enlists us to ensure that any reader (for example, the one we have at our disposal, ourselves) will obtain, for nothing . . . ; thus we are invited by the advertisement to make it true.

All of this happens as if words were not signs by nature: they need a little help. A single error, standing in the way of this help and demanding too much of it, has the power to rebuff it and reveals our cooperation here.

MARCUS AURELIUS'S RUSE

"*I have often asked myself in amazement,*" writes Marcus Aurelius, "*why each of us loves himself above all others and yet sets less store by his own opinion of himself than by the opinion of others. It is certain that if a God or a wise man were to come and command us never to conceive or to think anything inside ourselves without immediately expressing it outwardly, even shouting it out, we would not be able to bear it for a day. It is therefore true that we dread our neighbor's opinion of ourselves more than our own.*"

We will notice, in this line of reasoning, both the way forward and the sticking point. We have to admit, or the rest crumbles, that other people are basing their judgments—just as we are—on this same thought, and that this thought can therefore travel from the inside out, or the reverse, at whim. The words leave no mark on it. It is as if these words did not exist.

(I am guessing that an idea this acute, and under fire at every instant, was Marcus Aurelius's principal concern. Except that he wanted to get it past us by calling our attention to an amusing paradox.)

The usual views about lying or sincerity all assume the same basis: namely, that we speak our thought directly, without intermediaries, rather than speaking our words, whose connections and play might produce a thousand surprising combinations, according to various laws.

This is the cause of some curious sentiments: that, for example, of the duplicity of the liar who, in one and the same moment, morality presumes, thinks something true but says something false. All it takes is a little experience of lying in order to recognize this for a sorry illusion.

A PARADISIACAL LANGUAGE

Lautréamont, after calling Lamartine a stork and Jean-Jacques Rousseau a big mush-for-brains, is not content to debate whether to be a classic or a romantic—as have been sober-minded people for one hundred years. He boldly inquires if it is possible to speak:

"*Youth listens to the counsel of its elders. It has unlimited confidence in itself.*"

"*If Cleopatra's morality had been less abridged, the face of the earth would have been forever changed. But its nose wouldn't have become any longer.*"[2]

"*Man is an oak. There is nothing more robust in all of nature. The universe does not have to take up arms in order to defend him. A drop of water is not enough to save him.*"[3]

And so on and so forth. The touching game is not new, nor is it harmless: it implies precisely that sentences—and in particular the sort of sentences that we call, oddly enough, thoughts—and ideas are cut from the same cloth, such that it is enough to reverse the order of the words to turn their meaning inside out. A new maxim expresses something opposite the first, but which cannot fail to be just as insistent, just as compelling, since it is not a different one but the same.

It is a question, in the *Poésies,* of *reductio ad absurdum.* If language were what we think it is . . .

. . . and what Marcus Aurelius thinks it is. Or Victor Hugo, who calls words *the Word.* (If romanticism gets its image of the passions from Jean-Jacques, it is even more certain that it takes its confusion of words and ideas from Condillac.) This is where Lautréamont erects his infernal machine. "There is nothing," he says, "that is incomprehensible." It more or less follows that we need no longer bother with thinking: sentences will do it. A little fiddling from time to time makes them vary.

RHYME'S REASON

Atys, after tracing the variations of a word out from the Romans, speaks proudly of its true meaning: religion, he says, is the citizens' bond [*lien*], seeing that *religio* . . . (Thus he hopes to know the word and the thing better at the same time.)

But there is no need to go in search of Atys. Mire says: "*You are quite right to call them Protestants. They are always protesting.*" And Béril: "*Do you know why I can't stand cabinetmakers* [*les menuisiers*]*? Because they are a nuisance to me* [*ils me nuisent*]."[4] But is Béril only joking? I'm not so sure that Atys is being serious. And all the knowledge in the world confers, here, what authority to decide? If this or that word changed its meaning, it was in order to escape an initial error or confusion (thus we no longer use *traire* for "pulling" an image, or the hair or eyes from our head, but only milk from an animal).[5] If some other meaning changed, it was on account of a new confusion, a pun, with the result that the genuine etymology is going to give us less-accurate information about this word's meaning than the presumed one. (In like fashion, *legs* [legacy] does not get its signification from *laisser* [to leave], whence it comes, but from *léguer* [to legate], which it imitates.)

The fact remains that this etymology runs little risk—where it uses old, worn-out words—of being caught out. It uses none of those words that we can happen upon, a minute later, fitted with a meaning that is too different (as in the case of the pun). But this is already a question of proportion, and of success: and of the success precisely of this conviction, this desire—from which stem both the grammarian's analysis and Pythia's divine wordplays—for thoughts and words to be so confused with one another that there is no shred of word that does not retain, through thick and through thin, *its* shred of thought.

We speak readily of the seductions of rhyme: for want, perhaps, of reasons. We are not surprised to find, it is in perfect keeping with our remarks, that the purpose of this rhyme is to ground momentarily the claim laid by closely related sounds to closely related thoughts—and thus to flatter our preoccupation with a perfect language. We would by no means reproach rhyme, from time to time, for prejudicing meaning had we not been counting on it to help it along. If we experience this disappointment it is because we had this hope.

JACOB COW, THE PIRATE

Mac Orlan used to tell the story of how, when he fell, with his sailors and his Negroes, into Cow's clutches, the pirate lined them all up on deck. And then he went from one to the next:

"*What is your name?*"

"*Dick Smith, from Chicago.*"

"*Good. Into the sea with him.*"

They throw Dick Smith overboard. When it is Mac Orlan's turn, he says:

"*My name is Jacob Cow.*"

So great is the terror inspired by this name that Jacob Cow himself goes running back to his pirate ship, unfurls his sails, and is gone.

We deal with words as if Jacob Cow had to flee every time. Consequently there are forbidden words, those pertaining to devils and dangerous animals: *belette* pays a compliment, now the other name is lost.[6] Old diseases that are coming back are doing so under new names: two years ago the government censors banned any mention of the plague. And girls with whom we strike up a conversation refuse to tell us their names (for fear of granting us some hold over them). "*I never had the blues,*" says Alceus, "*before I knew this word.*" It is a strange standard, at every moment under fire, at every moment upheld: it is as if we could not stand to go on speaking if, for an instant, words stopped being signs for us, and such perfect signs that they must be confused with things. Cow, however, in actual fact does not flee. Béril is not seduced by the rhyme, any more than by the sugar advertisement: "That's a fast one," he thinks.

To be sure. And Marcus Aurelius's reflection is not the sort that cannot easily be refuted. Puns are hardly even considered. We may therefore observe that those cases in which we thought we were catching this confusion of words and things in the act were the same ones in which this confusion had threatened to come undone: as if it were alone its flaw, and already its fissure, that held our attention.

Our standard, too, to the same degree as this flaw, will show another side.

LANGUAGE FLATTERED

Mire talks, and lets himself talk. Effortlessly, he changes things around, moving cities, a cache of gold, a couple of days and nights closer together or farther apart. His tongue eventually slips, however, and we wonder: "Is *that word* really the one he wanted?" Or some listener complains. "We are not understanding each other," replies Mire. "You must understand *my words* better. . . ." Immediately words make an appearance, and in their capacity as signs: at this moment meaning is threatened, does not work, comes crashing down, with the result that we perceive thought on one side and, on the other, the lifeless word. Much as a tennis player who has just missed his shot looks in amazement at an arm or a racket that, a minute ago, were a part of him but are now alien and made of a stubborn material.

The idea of the sign bears, in addition to this reversal and precisely on its occasion, the stamp of a certain confidence. It informs us that words, despite appearances—and including the word that has just disappointed us—belong to thought, that they are going to make sense again. It is a practical idea, a defensive measure, and not the simple observation we might at first have believed. It says over and over: every thought has its word, every word its thought. Thus the coward says to himself, "How I am calm," and is emboldened.

The facts that we had at first opposed to one another are hereby brought together and reconciled. It is because they want to turn it into a sign, and win this victory over it, that Cilia and Atys make the word that disconcerts them the basis of some imagined thought, of which this word would henceforth be merely the outward appearance. Thus they protect themselves from a language that is dangerous or embarrassing as soon as it intrudes on our attention, so much so that we may fairly say that people speak and express themselves despite this language—rather than through it.

The practical man holds that all of humanity is made up of scoundrels. He adds that every scoundrel is good for something if only we know how to handle him. A similar wisdom governs our idea of the sign. I am willing to admit that it spares us some grave disappointments: and yet, overly suspicious, always anxious to imagine the worst, it neglects the most basic possibilities of words, their naive possibilities.

Two men meet: "How are things?—Ah! Sadoul has been sentenced to death." Or this young woman says to her lover: "What do you call me?—Georgette my dear, my golden Georgette.—How stingy! Is that all?" We must admire how their language achieves such reality from the outset. Whenever literary works, which ought to lay claim to a similar reality, or even a more independent one, seem nevertheless to be shy and retiring, people suggest that this is because these works have too quickly accepted this state of language, in which words continually show signs of falling short, as the ideal state. This is the only state of language taken into account by those doctrines holding that the writer expresses things or expresses himself, that sincerity is his guiding virtue and emotion his state of grace, all the more so if it is intense, and, they say, personal—things of this nature. It seems that, wanting to make the most of this strange occurrence, that words make meaning, we are condemned to grasp it in its weakest state and when it is coming unraveled. If we must ask a favor of someone, we wait until he is sick or of feeble mind. We flatter ourselves that he is in our power. But there comes a day when some phrase from him that is more ornery or stubborn makes it clear that he is doing better and getting away from us.

2.
CHASING AFTER IMAGES, OR, THE CHINESE TAILOR

We have done away with the old rhetoric, whereby we are now all obliged to make rhetoric our stock in trade. The risk is all the greater as everyone keeps his discoveries to himself, affording opportunity neither for comparison nor for critique. Instead of the pleasant variety we might have expected, we arrive at a monotonous abundance of principles that are all inaccurate, subject to the simplest illusions, and in particular to those illusions that further our concern to make use of words quickly.

This is the same principle that links the writer's labors to the discovery of new images. I am not saying it is more foolish than any other; it has served us well. And yet, it is singularly unconvincing as soon as it must give its reasons.

IF ALL WORDS WERE IMAGES

The theory that words are deadened metaphors has, as we know, met with unparalleled success. The critics have found in this theory proof of the doctrine they have cherished for some one hundred years.

"*It has been determined that the origin of the word* briller *[to sparkle, gleam, or glitter],*" writes Remy de Gourmont, "*is* beryllare, *which means to sparkle like beryl. What would the literature professors have to say if, now that* briller *really has nothing but an abstract meaning, some 'decadent' coined the word* émerauder *[to emerald] or* topazer *[to topaz]*?"

It is a question, here, of vindicating the decadents, elsewhere, the romantics. There is no image so bold, or so it seems, that the popular instinct has not imagined one bolder still, and *carried it off.* A professor finds it astonishing that Jules Renard writes: "*She flapped her little lizard arms. . . .* " The Latin tongue, with similar audacity, calls the muscular arm *lacertus, lizard,* because the shivering of the muscles under the skin can be likened to a lizard in motion.

We can in no wise speak, therefore, of language's functioning in two different ways. Rather, the procedure employed by the good writer is universal, or close to it. In the modern European languages, "almost all the words are metaphors." If we demand details or reasons, Bréal and Darmesteter offer us a long string of popular metaphors, which are a dime a dozen:

"To accost a passerby [accoster *un passant*]," "to tackle a question [aborder *une question*]," "to be thwarted in an enterprise [échouer *dans une enterprise*]"—these are so many metaphors that come from the sea. *Opportune, importunate* are images borrowed from the idea of an easy or more difficult coming ashore. *Travail* [work] implies first and foremost the image of a fettered and subjugated horse. A sound is deep [*grave*], a note shrill [*aiguë*], a house shady [*louche*].[7]

Indeed. We may conclude, from a thousand similar observations, that in none of the languages whose history we can study is there an abstract word, which, if we know its etymology, does not resolve into metaphor.

I do not disagree with any of this and accept that the cause lies in "the need we carry within us to represent and to paint what we feel in the form images." Bréal and Darmesteter forget only one thing, which is to show that we are indeed dealing with metaphors.

THE SCHOLARS' CRITIQUE

A cabinetmaker says about the legislation just voted on: "It still needs a good once-over with the plane." A photographer says: ". . . a little retouching." Both are thus using the simplest terms, the first to come to their minds, and that present them naturally with the idea of a finishing touch to be given some piece of furniture, negative, or law. Far from seeking metaphor out, they are trying to avoid it.

But this planing, this retouching, you say, produces an image. To be sure, for you who are not a cabinetmaker or a photographer. "It is simply a question," you add, "of writing a fair copy of the law." Well! Your fair copy is what is going to seem an image to the cabinetmaker.

In such cases metaphor, far from being the consequence of our "need to paint what we feel," translates a failure of understanding between the interlocutors. We take in what they are saying to us, through metaphor, in inverted form and on a different level. There exist subtler differences among men than those stemming from profession or custom: there is the difference of language, and differences, above all, of ease and confidence in the use of a single language. Thanks to which the field of false metaphor is made larger. It is no longer a question here of words that are "self-evident" to the speaker but strike the listener as mannered or affected. Even the words that the speaker discovers come to him from an unexpected direction.

A child or a foreigner speaks of a "spoon with holes," or of a "lid for the head." What fanciful notions, we think. This is because they do not know *fork* or *hat,* or else these words have escaped them. They are just trying to stay as close as possible to the object and to make themselves understood. (The image is in this instance produced for us by this spreading of *fork* in the direction of *spoon,* with which we are confronted. If *spoon* does not *produce* the same image for the child or the foreigner this is because they are reaching for the *fork.*)

We can hardly reproach the person who remarks, in such cases, "the curious image." But if he is inclined, later on, to express admiration at the child's or the foreigner's use of metaphor, we would do well to stop him and point out his illusion.

This illusion is not unlike an optical illusion. There can be little doubt that Bréal is taken in by it, and Darmesteter. The image is operative for these two linguists, who are considering, in a single moment, this modern and abstract word, *accoster* [to accost], and this other one, *côte* [coast], which is a different one and yet the same. It is operative *owing to this discrepancy,* as was the case above between *fork* and *spoon with holes* or, for the photographer, between *fair copy* and *once-over with the plane.* Bréal's only mistake is to assume that the Roman or the Frenchman of four hundred years ago used his language with such great knowledge and detachment.

CÉLINE AND THE KIKUYU

Céline marvels that the Kikuyu refer to the Milky Way as "celestial clinging vine" and to joy as "moonlight-of-the-heart," and she wants to live in this country. "What poets!" she says. But the civilized Kikuyu was excited to learn that his clinging vine was, for us, Milky Way: "Path of milk, what a lovely image, and what a pleasure to be among educated people." Céline was not thinking about the milk, just as the Kikuyu was not thinking about the vine.

The explorers Stanley and Gatschet observe of the Africans and Indians that they seem not to have a single idea but only images. I have enjoyed the company of elderly Malagasy men who had brought back with them from a voyage to Europe the same sentiment with regard to the English and French languages, and they did not scruple to express it. They drew from this conclusions as to the characters of the different races. And this mother who was saying a moment ago: "Where in Heaven's name does Jacques get these things? He tells me that he unscrewed the rainbow ball. What a poet! He means the glass knob on the banister."

We would do well to say to the mother, to Stanley, to Céline: "You see an image because you have not understood, and because of your hesitation. Rainbow ball is thus surprising to you. You try to grasp its meaning, and imagine everything there is about the rainbow before you come to the ball. But the child, *who starts off with this ball,* has never been so set against seeing a rainbow. In like fashion, Céline, you are the only one who sees the moonlight in a heart: the Kikuyu does not see it now, because he is used to the word. In olden days, he saw it even less because he was concerned to designate the thing and not get all confused."

We do not understand words directly, but rather according to the meanings we fashion for them. The presence of the image in this sense reveals a belatedness and a rupture of understanding—as if language had been short-circuited. We judge writers in the same way.

THE READER'S ILLUSION

We recently learned that the exotic poems that seem to us so extraordinarily rich in images turned out to consist, in truth, of an amassing of commonplace expressions and of proverbs, be they Malagasy *hain-teny* or Chinese *cheking*:

Oh! the delicate ones! Oh! the soft
Mists of dawn in the southern mountains!
Oh! the pretty ones! Oh! the charming
Young girls who hunger so!

The hunger, the mists of dawn here are not metaphors for the Chinese, or an original way of evoking the anguish of love, but rather this anguish given proper expression, as when lips are coral-red. Granet establishes this, and then adds:

"*The art of the songs is totally spontaneous: metaphors and similes remain, so to speak, absent. . . . One does not find those technical devices that reveal the art of our writers. . . .*"

I take this to mean that French poets, unlike Chinese, use technical devices: what are we doing here but transferring the error of which we had only just disabused ourselves to another literature. The same illusion is going to present us with these technical devices where they are not.

Albalat rightly recommends that we spend our time with those writers in whose work the effort to "make art" is visible. "*Rousseau,*" he says, "*whom we can catch in the act . . .*" and I am on guard. But "*at the top of the list of authors who let us see their devices, we must place Homer.*" The illusion has occurred. "*What I find astonishing,*" says Brunetière, "*is that people are taken in by this rhetoric.*" But he is talking about Baudelaire, and about the very things in Baudelaire that are not rhetoric: "Beauty," or "Invitation to the Voyage," rather than "Don Juan." This is because the reader of a poem naturally imagines the poet *as he would be* if by some chance he were the one writing the poem. Thus it seems to him that the difficulties, the surprises that the work sets before him were the writer's object and guiding intention. When the surprise is repeated, he cries "device." So much does an overly naive confidence in the natural virtue of words mislead him.

THE POETS' FLAW

A certain genius can distance the poet from us, as time did the ancient Roman, or space the Kikuyu. It would be tricky trying to specify its workings exactly. An inventor of language, this poet doubtless cannot be compared to the child in every respect, or to the man who tries his hand at speaking a foreign language for the first time. And yet he is equally misunderstood, and for the same reasons.

Taine applauds Homer for likening the wounded body of Menelaus to the ivory that the Carian women dip in crimson. Albalat admires Chateaubriand for writing "*. . . the nibbling of the rain on the hood of my carriage.*" As you wish. However, when Taine and Albalat endeavor to make an example of Homer and say: "*A good technique for finding images consists in . . .* " they plunge into the illusion headlong. For the fact is that Homer's true exertion had to be finding, beneath the ivory, or despite the ivory, a bloody body—and not the body leading to the ivory. If Chateaubriand discovers the rain, it is because he wants to rid himself of this nibbling. The most foreign thing, in other words, seems to them natural, and they are seeking the commonplace.

Do you think them so foolish as to hear the nibbling first or perceive only the ivory? It is the lot of poets to find the simplest acts inherently difficult. (It would be most advisable to work regular hours, recommends common sense.) But seeing is an act: the most difficult and complex. And to see what is there accurately, as it is—what an achievement. Is it really so surprising that the poet does not succeed on the first try? It is enough to extend just a little the observation that he has his head "in the clouds."

And the purest qualities of thought, too, remain unfathomable without some flaw that sets them into motion. The saints sometimes began by murdering their parents, or with some other quite extraordinary moral lapse. We do not slight the poet simply by seeing, at the origin of his work, a similar intellectual failing, which his metaphors, continuously overcome with errors, translate, or these difficult words endowed with meaning. For the poet, language retains its opacity, as the world, said André Gide, retains its thickness.

A Chinese tailor obtained permission from a servant to keep the queen's dress for a few days because he wanted to understand the intricacies of the cut. No sooner did he put it in his hut, however—he had no other place to store it—than it was eaten through by mites and moths, on account of the rare quality of the cloth. Afterward, the tailor painstakingly produced an imitation. But with utmost care he transferred the various holes to the new dress, thinking they held some secret. So it is that the poets who, deceived by words, go chasing after images and mistake as ideal the very flaw that the true poet went to great lengths to avoid. So it is with the treatises on the art of writing, and with Céline, and with the Kikuyu.

RHETORIC RISES FROM ITS ASHES
AND
YOUNG LADY WITH MIRRORS

Written in 1938, these two essays appeared in succession in the journal *Mesures* in that same year (January 15 and April 15, respectively). Paulhan composed both texts as he was feverishly completing a second (definitive) version of *Les Fleurs de Tarbes* (Paris: Gallimard, 1941), and already thinking about adding a second volume. (The first version appeared in serial form in the *Nouvelle Revue Française* from June to October 1936.)

Both "Rhetoric Rises from Its Ashes" and "Young Lady with Mirrors" are intimately related to Paulhan's project in *The Flowers of Tarbes* (see the introduction to this volume), and both treat at length the complex relationship between Rhetoric and Terror. Each, however, deserves to be read in its own right, placing its own emphases and elucidating Paulhan's theories of language with its own catalogue of figures and expressions. The two essays are included in the *Œuvres complètes*, volume 2, pp. 157–67 and pp. 171–83.

RHETORIC RISES FROM ITS ASHES

Translated by Jennifer Bajorek

When it comes to problems of style, we tend to think that there is something middling or base about them—and we hasten to dismiss them. If someone is going to dwell on my language, said Montaigne, I would rather he keep it to himself. "I am not a writer," says the writer. Here we are, blissfully returned to love, force, and fear—things in the world.

Of rhetorical problems. That they cannot be avoided, and that it is only our cowardice that paints them as middling or base.

Yet there is no avoiding that these bring us quickly back to language. For the ragbag of the intellect proves, in practice, to be full of artifice and apparent falsity. Of all the different events strung together in a novel, one seems improbable to us: this is the one that happened; of all the characters, it is the truest to life; of all the dialogues, the most faithful. A sure way not to convince anyone is to expose our thought, our emotion, as it is. Nothing seems as literary, in literature, as the authentic.

Whoever revisits the problem of rhetoric notices, to his surprise, that there is nothing quite so rigorous or so serious; he must commit himself to it entirely if he wants simply to understand it, and there is scarcely any solution here that does not resemble, that is not in essence, an oath. If he then recalls his initial distaste, he recognizes it for the effect of his weakness, and of the common cowardice that dissuades us from a task we find just a little too difficult, and paints it as wild or petty. Now he has nothing better to do than to eat those sour grapes.

He goes, to begin with, to the heart of the matter.

1.
THE LITERARY PARADOX

The *literary paradox:* it is a single expression, the commonplace, that seems, to Terror, the mark of bondage yet, to Rhetoric, of the liberation of the mind.

The modern world has curiously renounced rhetoric for the same reason that had created rhetoric. If we devised rules and genres in the first place, it was to guarantee the human spirit its full freedom, to allow it its cry, and wonder, and heartfelt song. And it is likewise to guarantee this song and these surprises that, today, we reject rules and endeavor to mix genres. If we invented three-pointed discourse or tragedy in five acts, it was to spare ourselves artifice once and for all. And it is likewise to spare ourselves artifice that, today, we shun three points or five acts. In fine, rhetoric, by its own account, has never proposed to do anything but rescue the writer from conventions and phrases: to bring him back to the natural, to truth. But it seems to us instead that it has never produced anything but concocters of phrases and arrangers of words. Hence, on one side, originality, rebellion, and Terror; on the other, obedience, imitation, respect for rules. The *literary paradox* is stranger still: it is that Terror's proofs and arguments are also Rhetoric's. It makes us think of some famous person whom some consider to be too skinny and others too fat. And that is not the half of it: they are looking at the same portrait. Even better: the same features of this portrait, the same curve of their cheek or their hip. For Rhetoric claims to free the mind from the influence of language—and the best proof it gives of its success is its use of rules and commonplace expressions. But an anti-rhetoric wants in its turn nothing more than to free the mind from its fetters of words. It calls these fetters by name: they are also commonplaces and rules.

Well, it cannot be both at once. If a cliché sets free the soul, it cannot enslave it at the same time. If a rule subjugates language to thought, it cannot at the same time make thought bow to language—not without being a thing so strange that one would have to abandon every other care in order to penetrate it. People sometimes say that men, and writers especially, have been known to change their tastes. But it seems instead that everything in the world changes except the tastes of men and writers.

Such is the central paradox of Literature. We will readily observe,

Of the everyday milieu where Rhetoric and Terror come into play. How thought is confused with language, and how it is distinct.

before attacking its difficulty, its fundamentally naive and obvious aspects. In truth it appeals to nothing other than our everyday experience, as if Literature constantly drew its matter and its ground from this experience, of which it would be nothing but a purer and more precise *state.* We can have the impression, when it comes to everyday conversation and reflection, that language does not appear to be wholly distinct from thought. But we cannot sort them out: in one case we are speaking our thought; in another, we are thinking our language. "How are you?. . . I don't like this cold weather. It is going to get even colder, the swallows have already flown. . . ." We need only enter the stream of everyday chatter to feel that it is not a question here, *particularly,* of words or of thought. The two go hand-in-hand.

Not that they cannot be separated at any moment. All it takes is some hesitation, a change of heart, a question that is never *perfectly* obscure: "The swallows, you *mean* the house martins? . . . Since you asked about my health . . ." Or: "This word you used . . . what if your words went beyond your intention?" Immediately the confusion dissipates, and we concede that there were, in fact, words *and* thought. And between them can arise any and every possible relation: fidelity and betrayal, vagueness and tightness, carelessness and precision. The commitment [*engagement*] and the release [*dégagement*] with which Terror and Rhetoric are connected are only one of these relations, and not the least familiar. It happens all the time that we are at a loss for a word, and we are searching for it, trying out ten words one after the other, each one close yet distinguished by some slight nuance of meaning: this one seems too ponderous to us, that one too free, and this other one pretentious. It sometimes happens that the forgotten word comes back to us at last, and we recognize it; sometimes it appears not to exist, and we stay stuck between several words, each of which seems abusive or clumsy—stuck, and so all the more promptly thrown back onto our pure thought. (It is the same way with dreams, when we try to recount them, with scant success.)

I am only trying patiently to find the everyday milieu where Terror and Rhetoric operate: it seems to us, in such cases, that each word risks *committing* us a little more than we would like. *Master of the word you are about to say, slave of the word you have said.* Nor are we at a loss for excuses, as soon as it is a question of shaking off our bonds: "The phrase went beyond my thought. . . . Don't take it literally. . . . It was only a manner of speaking . . ." and so forth.

Of the traits shared by Rhetoric and Terror: the commonplace as catalyst; thought preferable to language. Why we will look at Terror first.

We may note, in consequence, that Terror and Rhetoric are in agreement on two further points. One is that it is characteristic of rules and commonplace expressions to produce this dissociation of word and idea: or at least to precipitate it—not unlike the catalysts of this separation. It is, in any case, in connection with them that the question crops up, and that the opposite answers are given.

The second point is that both answers are inspired by the same principle; it is (roughly) that thought *counts for more* than language: that we must rely on it in the last resort. But we call for its choice, we request its decision, as if there were no greater humiliation than having to do language's bidding.

When all is said and done, it is acceptable to take sides. In some respects, by virtue of its authority and its obviousness, this partisanship reminds us of that other, purely moral, partisanship that rehearses the conflict of the body and the spirit and in the end demands the body's submission. Thus it is with language, that body of thought.

The fact remains that such partisanship may in its turn be expressed by two doctrines that are contradictory to the same degree. Here we are, faced with the paradox again. Only we should note that Terror presents us, as compared to Rhetoric, with a more promising terrain for its investigation.

For the latter is content to reel off its rules and its principles as if they were self-evident. Here we have metaphor and hypallage, it says, and over here the topics.[1] It adds (as if it were an afterthought) that this is how the student attains to truth, and to the purest reaches of the mind. Terror, on the other hand, sets out from a *view* of Rhetoric: to be precise, it sets out from a consideration of rhetoric's flaws, its errors, its pitfalls. It would not be enough to say that Terror is acquainted with Rhetoric: it proceeds from it and follows in its footsteps; Terror will never be done with knowing Rhetoric, and never done with refuting it. There is no evidence in the trial that it does not display and argue before us.

2.
RHETORIC IN FORCED RETREAT

The first side of the terrorist argument. Of *contrived* rhyme and cliché. In which the rhetorician seeks his bondage.

I imagine us in the midst of rhetoric: subject to rules and to genres, bound by this or that figure of speech, one sort of phrase or of word or another: metaphor, rhyming verse, the poetic word. These expressions are themselves subject to the topics they are supposed to render: comparison, the end, the means, the brevity of lovely days, the vulgarity of the crowd.

It is this subjection that Terror takes on. It finds, in Rhetoric's own confessions, sufficient grounds for its attack.

We are always hearing about the ill effects of rhyme or of metaphor. What? The poet must stop in mid inspiration and make concessions to a sound, a noise, an empty form, and put down three words where he had two in mind? How will his passion, his thoughts, remain authentic if he does? Here they are all deformed, counterfeited, letting nothing through to us in the end but a forgery, in which the writer's cunning gets all mixed up with the man's emotion. We would be only too glad if his humiliation could be kept secret, and if the counterfeit had the sheen of truth. But nobody is taken in. The drama has one act too many. The verse is full of fluff:

> Sire, I speak frankly, with no flattering dye.
> Yet more, we have no warlike enginery.[2]

and the topics follow suit:

> Virtue, when made the *first principle* of man, happily steers a *middle course* between the extreme vices and prepares us, through its soothing action, for the eternal *end*. . . .[3]

And even if we are taken in, there remains the shame of the poet or the orator, constrained by who knows what despotism to carve up and whittle away at his intoxication and his transport, or, conversely, to blow them up into a premeditated language machine. We have heard our share about the battle of the angel and the aesthete, the gallon and the amphora, poetry and beauty. Or, if you prefer, of the young romantic and the classicist getting on in years.

For the objection is an ancient one. And the response—if, that is, we are not going to abandon the poet to his lying and his forgeries—is no less ancient. (And yet they are both so *natural* we hardly guess their age.)

The second side of the terrorist argument. Of *natural* rhyme and cliché. In which the rhetorician is no longer even aware of his bondage.

"I didn't *mean* it," says the classicist. "It sometimes happens, of course, that I must proceed by trial and error. Even then I do not always find the right topic, or the right rhyme. And indeed, often those parts of my verse that, to you, seem artifice or labor are those that have come to me from the gods. Frequently, the rhyme reaches me before the idea, or at least all confused with it, and the words all confused with my emotion. Thought and language are, for me, a seamless whole. And just as you talk all the time about a tree or the sky without being the least bit conscious that you are using the word *tree,* or *sky,* so it is, for me, with meter and assonance. Rhyme is my grammar; metaphor, my syntax."

So says the rhetorician. Someone objects that this is not a matter of common experience, and he will likely fire back that he would not be a poet if he were himself entirely common: that the terrorist furthermore has his own keywords and rhymes; it is simply that he uses them, because he refuses to acknowledge them, without any tact. Victor Hugo boasts, in more than one place, of having made mincemeat of rhetoric and having made hypallage tremble. But his poems are full of *battoirs vertueux* [virtuous cudgels], *gerbes généreuses* [generous bundles], *lins candides* [blameless linen], *herses fidèles* [loyal portcullises]. Delille showed more restraint.

The terrorist has his ready reply. "That may be," he says. "Did I ever claim we were perfect? It is just that your bondage, and sometimes our own, date back so far that we can no longer see them clearly. Is one any less a serf through being ignorant of his servitude? They tamed you, at an early age, with these vain sonorous figures. You *learned,* as one learns another language, rules and commonplace expressions, tropes and manners. Are they any less a habit through seeming natural to you now? Any less conventional through seeming spontaneous? You are in even worse shape than I thought. For technique and artifice would at least have left you some intellectual freedom, and an awareness of your fall. But you yourself have become rhetoric and language."

Thus we see every one of rhetoric's arguments turned against it. If the topics seem contrived, it is because the mind agrees to yield to language; if they seem natural, it is because it has succumbed to language once and for all. And the presence of the rule or the commonplace betrays only servitude and submission at every turn.

There you have them, Terror's reasons. We must admit that they command attention. What is more, they seem so easy, so glibly conjured, that we ought perhaps to be surprised that Rhetoric has withstood them for so long. (We did not need to wait for Victor Hugo to come along to invent them. No, Plato and Montaigne, Pascal and Diderot were forever offering the same objections to the adepts and eloquents of their time.) Still, one has to wonder whether they are not a little too easy. There exist doctrines that are hampered by nothing: they are not always the soundest, or the best founded. And then, I can see all too clearly the extremes to which this one would have to be taken: to the point of maintaining that all syntax betrays the spirit, and all language lies. For if it seems mannered, we cry artifice; and we cry servitude if it seems spontaneous. (But it is possible, after all, and who am I to say, that we will have to renounce language.) There is worse.

Logical weakness of the terrorist argument. The attempt to reduce every expression to its linguistic element betrays little more than partisanship.

The fact is that we may turn Terror's reasons around quite easily, employing the same mode of argument in order to defend words, rules, or commonplace expressions. If they seem natural (so we will think), it is because the mind has been given free rein, because the rule has ceased to be opaque and formulaic for it; and the mind has gone beyond the rule to find its proper laws.—But it can happen that you were looking for them.—Granted. I do not *use* these laws, though, until they have been improved by the mind. Then I no longer perceive their words, but only that part of them that consists of thought. . . .

It is only too easy to turn every one of Terror's arguments against it in this fashion: if the commonplace expression seems spontaneous, this is evidence of a gain on language. If it seems mannered, we are witnessing the victory of the mind.

Everyone knows that card trick where the subject is led to pick the card that the illusionist had chosen already. (For example, the seven of diamonds.) "Will you take the red or the black?

—The black.—Fine. There are only red cards remaining. Hearts or diamonds?—Diamonds.—Very well then, from the red cards, the face cards or the lesser ones?—Face cards.—I'll let you have them. And from the lesser cards. . . ."

The ruse is sometimes successful. The trick with which we are concerned is hardly more subtle. Only it appears that the terrorist and the rhetorician, having *first* made a choice between language or thought, agree to understand every example concerning them in accordance with this partisanship. (There is, moreover, not an expression in the world that does not have *its* language and *its* thought.) We must dismiss the adversaries.

3. IN WHICH RHETORIC MAKES A VIRTUE OF ITS VICE

In which it is acknowledged that Terror is a state of mind that is routinely provoked by Rhetoric.

Hollow or mediocre as Terror's argument may be, as naive its ambition, the fact remains that it happens. This is not saying enough: it is a *common* occurrence. It is, for want of proof, a state of mind. Who has not said to himself, upon hearing an electoral speech or a street-hawker's patter: "Those are only phrases he is rattling off . . . does he really think he's going to con me with these slogans?" Even if it is only to think a moment later: "Really now! He has already said all these things a dozen times. . . . It is quite possible he has come to believe them. . . . He doesn't even see that these are words anymore." We thus move effortlessly from one position in the argument to another, as if they were in fact only a single thought whose two sides we were discovering in succession.

We know, regarding this thought, that it comes *routinely* into play wherever there is rhetoric; that it follows from it and is akin to its second stage. We have said that Terror *comprehends* rhetoric. But when the rhetor says, repeatedly, that we must not leave the compass in the circle, or the yardstick in the wall, and that true rhetoric begins with a feeling of disgust for rhetoric (just as philosophy begins with hatred of philosophy), what does he do but predict Terror in its turn and already comprehend it? If Montaigne knows Cicero, Cicero is expecting Montaigne.

Here we are, having arrived gradually at a new problem having less to do with the extent than with the *nature* of Terror. The question is no longer, "What does the terrorist want?" but rather, "What is he thinking?" Not: "What is rhetoric that it warrants so many conflicting grievances at once?" but, "Who is the terrorist if all these conflicting grievances seem, to him, the same one? If he uses them all indiscriminately. . . ." I have said that Terror is an everyday occurrence. This is not to say that it is simple, far from it. But for whoever is seeking to know less what good it is than what it *is,* two distinct features are immediately clear.

One is that the terrorist vacillates between two *phrases* that are *essentially* different, prepared at every moment, on the least information, to go from one to the next. The first, cobbled together in the moment, is a clever construction, the height of cunning and technique. The second is naive and artless, ready-made, spontaneous, without a trace of artifice joining its elements, without the least little suggestion of intention. It has all the incongruity of an emerald in reinforced concrete, a piece of coal in a brick. And of course the *apparent* phrase has not changed in any way. It is still the *je ne farde guère* ["I speak with no flattering dye"], the *battoir vertueux* [virtuous cudgel], the *éperon pur* [noble spur]. This is precisely because Terror had no greater hope than to transcend appearance. The French word *louer*[4] looks a lot like two words, *locare* and *laudere* (just as *dé* looks like both *datum* and *digitale*). Properly speaking, it is two words—it has *two essential natures*—but everyday consciousness makes no mistake here, any more than the scholar. It is just that the terrorist must ask more painstakingly whether "virtuous cudgel" is a phrase that is fabricated or spontaneous, artificial or natural. He makes use in this case, as we have seen, of the least little hint. He runs off after the faintest scent. This searching or this doubt, betrayed by his objection, has a second feature.

The terrorist vacillates between two *phrases* that are *essentially* different, finds himself all the more promptly thrown back onto his thought. Here Terror appears as if it were Rhetoric's intention.

It is that he is himself driven back, on the basis of these doubts and this indecision, to a thought that is as free of words as possible. A thought *before* language, if there is such a thing, since it is not yet guaranteed language. Since it is *about this language* that the terrorist has doubts.

A person who is trying to choose between a silk dress or a wool one, a felt hat or a leather one, will invariably give some thought to the use and the reason for this hat or this dress. She thus retraces her steps to the intention. It is the same with the person who hesitates between two words and retraces his steps to the thought. Ordinarily it seems to us that we are touching a table, a banister, a hand with our fingers. However, when our sense of touch surprises or disorients us (such as when a piece of bread feels like two clenched between our fingers), touch slips immediately from our hands: it is our mind alone, we think, that was deceived. Thus it is with both the poet and the critic, neither of whom wonders whether this *battoir vertueux* is contrived or divinely inspired beyond the moment of its first revelation and the shock of deep thought it gives them.

Here we have our terrorist in the flesh: he is the one who goes back to thought on account of the commonplace, the figure of speech, or the trope, even as they give him cause to hesitate about the phrase—in exactly this way has Rhetoric been painting us, in the terrorist, a portrait of its writer. This discovery is strange but not inexplicable. It is not enough for us to recall, at this point, that rhetoric *portrays* this writer. If Terror is the state into which Rhetoric plunges us, but also the state that Rhetoric announced to us in advance, then probably it is, rather than the consequence or the effect of Rhetoric, its intention.

That Rhetoric unfolds in an added dimension as compared with Terror: it anticipates the objection to the rule; but it also anticipates the mentality that raises the objection.

We have said that Rhetoric, too, in all likelihood comprehends Terror. But it seems that it *comprehends* it in a more particular sense. When a hunter comes home soaking wet and freezing, the first thing he does, if he is sensible, is change his clothes. Then he lights his kitchen stove so he can cook his quail (because he is hungry). After that he switches on his radio so he can enjoy himself a little. This is what the hunter does if he is simply sensible. But if he has genius, he lights a roaring fire that dries him, roasts his quail, and is pleasing to look at at the same time.

Perhaps we should distinguish in like fashion between a literature of the roaring fire and a literature of the kitchen stove and dry clothes. For Terror is sensible when it anticipates the immediate objection that bristles in us at every rule or every cliché. It goes straight to the heart of the matter. It spares us a disappointment, which it accepts in advance. But Rhetoric anticipates the disappointment, and it anticipates Terror as well. Terror knows that man needs to dry his clothes; but Rhetoric knows that he *also* needs to eat and to enjoy himself. The terrorist knows something of literature; but the rhetorician knows something of literature and of the man who makes it. He sees things (as in a game of chess) one move ahead of the terrorist. In short, the merit of Rhetoric may well be this: that it *permits itself* Terror.

We may now make out between these two descriptions, whose disparity leads to the literary paradox, less a substantive opposition than a difference in scope. Except that the one—the terroristic one—is connected with a two-dimensional mentality, which raises the objection and leaves it at that: a mind totally distinct from its works, and which can be seen abstractly. Rhetoric, on the other hand, counters the objection and the mentality that made it—thus unfolding in another dimension, in which the relations between thoughts and words are reasserted. Raising the objection leads merely to a dismissal of the topics and the rules, but *being* the objection leads, by dint of a little more knowledge, to their rediscovery and reinvention—with a force that is all the greater as they were nearly lost. People sometimes assume that Rhetoric is addressed to simple minds. But probably we are the ones who have grown a little too simple to understand Rhetoric. We sometimes say that poetry is a more tragic and profound thing than imagined by those who would reduce it to meter, to caesura, or to rhyme. But it is possible that what made this reduction to meter and to rhyme possible in the first place was that they had *already* formed a deeper and more tragic consciousness of them.

That Rhetoric (as distinct from what we find with morality or philosophy) is itself the rhetorician.

We have known since Socrates that philosophy has a great many merits but a single flaw: namely, that it is not philosophical. No more than aesthetics is itself aesthetic, or morals moral. But each of these doctrines is achieved *elsewhere*, in the foreign and resistant material it exercises: they are made of madness and wisdom, beauty and horror, good and evil. (Philosophers understand this, and call themselves not wise, but lovers of wisdom.)

Must we not therefore try to fathom what it would take to have, on the contrary, a morality that would be enough to make the reader moral, an aesthetics that would make him beautiful, a philosophy that would make him wise? These are not mere chimeras. For Rhetoric (if, that is, our analysis is correct) is precisely that science which requires, if we are going to understand it, *a rhetorical event.* And which, without one, remains perfectly impenetrable.

Hence, in all likelihood, the distaste, the hesitation, the weakness we noted at the beginning: for the fact is that we must commit ourselves to it—and take the risk.

I said the weakness. And all the different passions that accompany and disguise it. Sometimes we are surprised that Literature seeks, these days, less coherence and precision than emotion, violence, trembling, with abandon. But doubtless there was a time, which it is up to us to remember, when Literature was quite confident of transforming us without endeavoring so much to move us; when it was too efficacious to have need of an *effect*. Which is why we can hardly see anything anymore, in all of these fits and agitation, but bad conscience over this lost efficacy.

YOUNG LADY WITH MIRRORS

Translated by Charlotte Mandell

There are some solutions that are even stranger than their problems. The problem at least was only *one* question; but the solution poses a thousand more. Indeed, we have found the reason for the literary paradox:[1] it is that the terrorist is himself that pure spirit, infinitely free of language, summoned by the rhetorician. Hence Terror and Rhetoric are both justified, one to say what it says, the other to be what it is. A curious difficulty remains.

That we have shifted the literary paradox rather than resolved it.

Common sense bids me to acknowledge that hesitating between particular words, wavering, changing heart, and continually weighing one's words, reveal the play of a thought that is purer of language than usual, because it has not yet found, but is still seeking, its expression: a way of thinking *before words,* if such a thing is possible. With the same obviousness, I *know* what that man is thinking as he paces back and forth at the crossroads, and sometimes chooses the road on the right and sometimes the one on the left; or that other person who, on the brink of a precipice and already feeling himself falling forward, cannot decide which of two tufts of grass to cling to. This obviousness, though, has another aspect: a face of shadow and paradox.

That is because we had to *guess* at the thinking of the terrorist. We have deduced it from his various statements. But we do not *witness* it. Even more, it seems that the terrorist himself remains powerless to discern it, to know it (for he persists in his claim). And what, after all, is a thought in us of which we are not aware, if not a simple cloud? We seem in fact to be limited to substituting a new paradox for the old one, and to shifting the difficulty rather than resolving it.

THE MACHIAVELLIANISM OF RHETORIC

Rhetoric's secret: it is not possible to offer an objection to it that does not enter into its plan.

Society said about Mme. Camoin that her prestige stemmed from the contradiction into which she plunged friends and adversaries alike, busy with blaming her either for her excessive gentleness or for her fierceness, her stubbornness or her carelessness; hence they were forced to recognize in her some secret that surpassed both gentleness and violence, insouciance and willpower. Chesterton said of Christianity, in the same sense, that after reproaching it for being too optimistic, but also too despairing; too tender, but also too brutal; too detached, but also too practical, its enemies would finally have to wind up confessing that it is exactly *this* that urges to the limit violence as well as gentleness, optimism as well as pessimism, and gives each its true color.

Thus one would have to say that Rhetoric derives its virtue from the confused mass of objections it provokes. "I write without any order," says one person, "and as things come to me; to give order to emotion is to lose it." "I *apply myself* to writing without order," says another: "the first draft is nothing but convention." Thus we reject Rhetoric, in the first instance, because it is artificial, and in the second, because it is natural. "It is pure contortion, and the mind is warped by it." "It is pure naiveté, the mind follows its own bent through it."

It is objected to, but praised as well. "I bend the incessant flight of my thinking to fixed rules," says one. "I thus give it an origin and an end—an existence." But the other: "Through rules, I restore to my mind its natural rhythm and weight." Thus we also praise Rhetoric, just as we blamed it earlier, for what is natural and for what is artificial about it, for the way it suits the intellect and for the way it resists it.

But for whoever keeps in mind *at the same time* both praises, and both rebukes, it would seem that Rhetoric possesses a secret that surpasses artifice and nature, the deliberate phrase and the rough one. In short, one cannot make any comment about it *that does not enter its plan.*

Before I approach it openly, I seek only to *popularize* the rhetorical problem. We sometimes say that some feeling has become real because we believed it. But about Rhetoric, conversely, we would have to say that it becomes real to the extent that we do not believe it: thanks to these fumblings around it, and these *various* rejections. Nor can we say that it tells a lie to get at the truth. Rather, more precisely, that it pretends to tell a lie to provoke the truth. "She reproached me," said Rousseau, "for being too bold, in order to have me understand that I could be even more so." This is Rhetoric, in the manner of courtesans. As if there were no combination of language to which the mind could not reply through new inventions.

It is a commonplace of the law that it is not enough to make new laws to prevent disputes and wars; on the contrary, obscurities are multiplied by the very commentaries offered about them, and difficulties increase the more they are anticipated. Now commentaries and anticipations in turn engender new court trials that are added to the others. Thus it is with Rhetoric, which offers no rule that is without exceptions. If a tyrant is interested in trials *for their own sake,* he should have every interest in multiplying laws. But who is not interested in Literature *for its own sake?* Accordingly, its precepts, conventions, unities are rightly multiplied. Certain subjects will be forbidden. The novelist (for instance) will have the right to talk about love—but not about money. The playwright, about friendship, and family sentiments, but under no pretext whatsoever should he discuss daydreams or health. Certain turns of style, certain metaphors, will be allowed, and others forbidden. The subtlest rhythmic combinations will be appropriate. Just as two people who use the same language do not lose their own souls by doing so but rather bring them to expression, so it is with two authors who speak through their subjects and chosen themes: *Phedra* distinguishes Racine from Pradon; *Amphitryon* shows the difference between Molière and Plautus. If Rhetoric was invented in the first place, it was surely to shed light on the personalities of writers. If it recommended (with such a gentle insistence) not even *trying* to be personal, it was the better to observe to what extent *one could not avoid being so.* Finally, it obstinately invited each writer to dance, as they say, in chains.

The young village girl: that Rhetoric, quite clear in its effects, is rather less so in its principle.

But we should not let this image mislead us. It might even be that it is exciting to dance in chains. I have never *seen* anyone manage it (or else the chains were fake); and of the writer himself, if I finally have to admit that the constraint serves him and thrills him, it is difficult for me to imagine in what way. So long as I remain uncertain on this point, Rhetoric is incomprehensible to me—at the mercy of the first argument that comes along. Here is the coarsest one. Pascal reproaches poets for having invented certain strange terms that they call poetical beauty: *golden age, marvel of our times, rosy lips.* "But" (he adds), "if you imagine a woman in such a manner, saying little things with big words, you'll see a pretty young village girl, adorned with mirrors. . . ."

It is too easy for Voltaire or Dacier to reply that *rosy lips* or *golden age* are neither "big words" nor constrained phrases, but the naive expression of surprise and delight. We in our turn will conclude that the phrase *rosy lips* should summon the purest thought, at the intersection of two languages, one that allows both for Pascal's opinion and Voltaire's. But I would like to have a clearer idea of this thought.

In fact, now we are thrown back onto our first difficulty. I will not approach it head-on. But I will try first of all to restore its amplitude and breadth, by means of parallel examples.

That it is in the nature of certain thoughts, if not all of them, that we are not able to observe them.

Who truly knows what he is thinking? Phédon thinks he hates Junie, but it is the beginning of a great love affair. Hermas thinks he is indifferent to Lélia: that is because he is much too responsive to her. Claude thought he was grateful to Celse, who saved him; but he is delighting in a death that carries away both Celse and gratitude. Moralists readily admit that the heart has to be learned, like a language.

There is an acute form of error. At every instant we are dealing with feelings that are impossible, or at least difficult, for us to observe in ourselves. The preacher who said, "As to modesty, I yield to no one," was mocked. But we have to separate out the paradox, hidden by the jest: namely, that it is contradictory to be modest, and to *know* that one is modest. For modesty consists in diminishing oneself. But if you *know* that you are diminishing yourself you also know that you are actually greater than you seem. So you stop being modest. Thus it is, conversely, with pride. You can say roughly that pride consists of giving yourself importance.

But if you *see* that you are exaggerating your importance, you stop exaggerating it. Seeing yourself as proud is the proof of modesty; seeing yourself as modest, of pride.

Thus it is with many other states of mind, and of thought. Goodness, devotion, consist in doing this or that—and in *not knowing* that you are good or devoted. If the hero discovers his courage and the gravity of the danger that is threatening him, he immediately stops being a hero and becomes a suicide. Space, time, civilization are clear ideas to us so long as we do not look at them too closely: but as soon as they are evoked, suddenly they become clouded and obscured—inexpressible as soon as one tries to express them, incapable of being grasped when you try to grasp them. And far from the *rhetorical state* being an exception to this, we should rather say that it follows the destiny of all thought.

The fact remains that this destiny has a characteristic that is stranger than it is common, and to it we feel less resigned—namely that courage, time, or modesty were simple ideas or feelings *without pretension,* which we too naturally think deranged by our attention. But Rhetoric had made us a promise, which it does not keep. It should have, if we are to understand it, revealed to us authentic spirit, pure thought. How could this be, if, when it takes its first step, it stumbles on a banal obstacle?

2.
WE CANNOT WITNESS OUR THOUGHTS WITHOUT CHANGING THEM

We are only ever able to grasp a diminished thought of ourselves.

It is interesting that the unconscious, as psychologists and psychoanalysts portray it to us, is usually just a *fortuitous* unconscious. It is a matter of thoughts, worries, obsessions, that could just as easily be conscious if some social taboo did not come and obstruct them: laws, conventions, scruples.

But now we are forced, on the other hand, to imagine a *natural* unconscious. For that matter, the simplest—but most obvious—remark should have led us to this point right away.

Namely, that thought alone can let us know thought. To be aware of any idea, anxiety, or feeling, is first of all to *withdraw* from them that share of thought necessary to our investigation. We never see them in their pure state; we never reflect—reflection being thought too—except on a thought denuded of this reflection. A man can no more grasp his mind *intact* than he can directly see the nape of his neck or his throat. There are, however, mirrors for seeing the back and front of the neck. But there are none for the mind. It is possible that original thinking has its unknown powers, its mysterious connections, its extreme freedom. But men know nothing of this—I am not speaking just about psychologists or philosophers (who seem to have given themselves the task of reassuring us about this) but about anyone at all, the man in the street, you and me. And surely there is no anxiety more haunting than the one that stems from this ignorance, judging solely by the tales and myths it troubles. Elsa wants to know who Lohengrin is, and Lohengrin disappears. If Psyche sees Love, Love vanishes. If Lot's wife turns back, she becomes a pillar of salt; Orpheus looks at Eurydice, and Eurydice returns to the Underworld. Precautions do nothing to change this: as swift as the glance is, as slight the turn of the head, everything is already over. I will not linger over these amusing concerns, which among us take the place of myths: the dog who chases his own tail, the cat who wants to catch hold of his shadow; the man obsessed by the desire to see himself, if only just once, as if he were someone else—the most naive or subtle legends also warn us that what is closest to us is the best hidden. Every man secretly carries within himself, so long as his life lasts, the invisible lover who was given to Psyche.

Of some devices for approaching our authentic thought.

But legend also prevents us from giving up. We are still surprised that the torch (as the proverbs say) does not illumine its handle, that the gaze can never be grasped by the gaze, and that man "knows everything but himself." It is unbearable for us that Orpheus cannot see Eurydice. And it is possible that our obsession with another *country*, an unknown country, does nothing but in its own way express the preoccupation we have with *our* unknown country, the only one forbidden us. But that it is forbidden to us *forever*, that at least we cannot accept.

Here, we can imagine more than one method or one investigation. The most "natural" ones, the ones that come to mind first, fail: neither haste or extreme suddenness, nor negligence, absence, or obliteration teach us in the end anything beyond our ordinary thoughts. It would seem, rather, that dream or daydream, automatic writing, deep song, cries, come to intensify even more the common processes of our conscience: more deliberate than reason, more calculated than our calculations, more literary than literature, and always up to date. Why should we be surprised at this, since we do not at all see why thought that observes is necessarily swifter than the thought observed; or the secret thought becomes obvious when the familiar thought vanishes. It has been said that there is only one kind of thought, to which our desire for a solution lends various qualities, depending on the case; and turning around even faster will not give the dog any more chance of catching his tail.

Where the direct way is ineffective, there remain indirect ways. It has been said that it would be enough for a man, for him to know himself, patiently to observe his conduct and his actions. That is possible; but I do not really see what such an observation could teach us that was new. If I even admit that my behavior *resembles* my deepest thoughts and reveals them more precisely than my reflection does (which is not at all proven, and seems to me scarcely probable), the fact nonetheless remains that it is still through reflection that I grasp this conduct. So that the same distortion, which I mistrusted, will be at work here—and all the more freely because a first *expression* has every chance of leaving it with a thought whose integrity is already threatened, if not forever compromised. One can dream, here, of a more effective method.

There is one point, at least, that we cannot help but take for granted: it is that our reflection—since it keeps pace with our actual thinking, and is of the same nature—at least is not completely deceived. That is because it grasps a part of the original thought—deprived of its own nuance and its essential characteristic, perhaps, and distorted too. But at least it is some portion of the thought, such that one could, starting from it—if one managed to know of *what* the distortion consists, and of what characteristic the reflection deprives it—reconstitute the original thought. It would be enough to observe *elsewhere* the play unique to reflection and the nature of the distortion it entails. By "elsewhere," I mean in some thought we were given to grasp *before* and *after* reflecting, so that this distortion was found to be multiplied. It is enough to pose the problem, though, to glimpse a solution.

Of translation: and that every alteration unique to a language is multiplied in it.

There is a characteristic of every translation, to which I am not sure we have ever given enough attention: it is—to put things in the simplest way—that it expresses some feeling or thought that had *already* received its expression. So that even though the translator tries to forget the words of the original text so as to retain only their spirit, and as passionately as he wants to be penetrated by the impressions he receives from them, he cannot completely neglect the word, and the attentive reader remains free to compare one text with the other at any moment. But this confrontation takes on a singular value, to our mind.

For if there is a characteristic unique to expression *as such*—for instance, a certain *alteration* it brings to thought—we have to admit that the alteration will, in the second text, be found to be *multiplied.* I will leave aside the chances for error that can be at play here. I will take the strictest, most faithful translation possible: it will have to present, in our hypothesis, in strict proportion to its faithfulness, a *systematic difference* from the original text, which will be the actual mark of expression. So that there would be nothing left to us—if we want to go back from the original text to the pure thought it expresses—but *to discover in it and capture a difference of the same nature.*

And we can simply be careful to choose a kind of translation where this difference has the chance of being clearly articulated: either it is a case of two languages of a very different structure, as with a civilized language and a primitive language; or of one single language, in two stages of its existence, in two places of its use, where the slightest discrepancy is brought out: thus standard contemporary French, compared with slang, and with the French of the sixteenth century.

It is enough to ask the question to find the answer: there is no attempt to translate Kikuyu or Cherokee into current French (or into English or German for that matter), the slang of butchers or cutpurses into literary French, or the language of the sixteenth century into that of the twentieth, that does not make us imagine, from one language to the other, a difference in *nature,* so clear and striking it could form the subject of more than one serious study: namely, that the language being translated—slang, Cherokee, or the language of Villon—seems to us at once more *imagistic* and more *concrete* than the language into which we are translating it.

3.
OF A WAY THAT LEADS TO AUTHENTIC THOUGHT

The language that we are translating seems more imagistic or more concrete to us than our own.

Victor Hugo said that ordinary French is limited to naming things, but that slang shows them. One example he gave of this is *lancequiner* (to rain), where the raindrops, he said, are fortuitously compared to the *lances* of the *lansquenets,* infantrymen. *Tête* [head] is just an abstract word to us, but *bille* [mug], *boule* [bowling ball], *trognon* [apple core], *fiole* [flask], *cafetière* [coffeepot], or *calebasse* [calabash] create images. *Babillarde* [chatterbox] is more expressive than *letter; faire du boniment* [give a sales pitch] more expressive than *win the favor of,* and so forth.

Many other languages should be quoted here besides slang. For a long time we have acknowledged, on the strength of Diderot and Rousseau, that savage peoples and children used an entirely poetic language. We still at times claim this today. When little Jacqueline says that the swans *plow* [*labourer*] the water and that her brother speaks *à tâtons* ["by touches," that is, gropingly, haphazardly], her family is overcome with admiration. But the *furrows* of water, *head,* or *good graces* would not seem any less imagistic to us, if habit had not erased their vividness for us. The same habit, though, hides from the child or the cutpurse the metaphor he is using: *mug* or *noggin* are no less abstract to him than our *head; babillarde* is as abstract as our *letter.* As for *lancequiner,* only Hugo, carried away by the translator's illusion, can discover a metaphor in it. The word is an ordinary derivative of *ance* (*eau,* water).[2]

The illusion can take on yet another form. Primitive language seems to us more concrete than our languages. From time immemorial we have spoken of the naiveté of the ancient authors, their respect for the slightest details, their ineptitude in dealing with the abstract. Explorers, for their part, admire the fact that the Laplanders have no general word for *reindeer,* but a particular word for a year-old reindeer, another for a two-year-old reindeer, another for a three-year-old reindeer, and so on. The Ugandans have no word for *arm,* but one word for the right arm and another for the left.

It is easy to counter that French says *poule* [hen], *poulet* [chicken], *poussin* [chick], or *coq* [rooster], but like the Laplander has no word for the species to which these various animals belong (which does not at all mean that it cannot form an abstract idea of it). That English distinguishes between *loving* God and *liking* potatoes but has no word (like Malagasy or French) that serves both sentiments. Whence it follows readily that the Ugandan or the Laplander, in turn victim of a recurrent illusion, will see in French or English a language that is concrete to excess. But the error matters less to us than the illusion.

That the translation dissociates the stereotypes of the original text.

It is curious that the mind is slower than the hand or the eye to overcome its natural illusions. The black dot we see in the distance is not a grain of dust or a dwarf, but a man, like us. We know it: we think we *see* a man. But we continue to aver (and more than one serious book deals wholly with this subject) that slang and exotic languages are imagistic and concrete, while our own language is thoroughly abstract. If I look for the reason for such a constant illusion, here is what I find: it is that any translation, all the more so the more faithful it is, has as its first effect that of *dissociating the stereotypes* of a text. It restores their independence to the elements of meaning linked in the original language. If I read casually:

Beaux enfants vous perdez la plus
Belle rose de vos chapeaux[3]

[Beautiful children you lose the most
Beautiful rose from your hats]

I can accept a vague feeling of some loss or decay, and be content with that. If I am a translator, or a meticulous commentator, I will remember first of all that there was once a fashion for flowered hats, even in the most serious social circles. Starting from that, I will explain that the most beautiful rose in the hat designates here, metaphorically, the most precious possession. Then my translation is done well enough to give the feeling of a language that is at once imagistic and concrete. But where is the image, the concrete? In this translation alone, and in the operation by which I return its detailed sense to a half-obscured sentence. A contemporary of Villon would have heard only a simple cliché, which would roughly be for us: "He lost the flower of his youth, the flower of his years." Thus *babillarde* [chatterbox], *bille* [mug], *labourer* [plow], *renne d'un an* [year-old reindeer], *bras droit* [right arm] do not give the feeling of anything concrete or of an image *except in the course of the process that translates them.* But our *head,* our *furrow,* our *rooster* and *hen* will seem to the primitive person, to the child, or to the cutpurse, images and concrete details. That is because they have to begin by breaking them up into concrete details, and creating images for them, thus building an entire sentence, almost a little fable.

I am not reminding translators here of anything that is not already current practice. When André Gide observes, in reading the *Thousand and One Nights,* that J.-C. Mardrus's translation, while no doubt unfaithful to the storyteller's mode of thinking, restores to us the very spirit and imagination of the Arabic language;[4] when Paul Mazon, writing about translations of the *Iliad,* notes the insurmountable difficulty that by translating Homeric phrases in their concrete detail, one breaks the natural rhythm of the text,[5] they do nothing but mark the distortion inherent to every translation—for which it is finally time to find a remedy.

How it would be possible to correct the distortions introduced by the translation and by consciousness.

That any reflection, however, acts on our original thinking in the same way that translation alters a text, I need no other proof than common consent. We currently acknowledge that analysis dissects and petrifies our impulses, our emotion. Thus Lot's wife becomes salt, and the Gorgon's visitor turns to stone. There is no myth that does not show upon our soul, *as soon as we look at it,* dispersion and ice. And Paul Mazon speaks of the translated *Iliad* in the same way the old mythologies describe Love—as soon as Psyche looked at him, he fled away. Except perhaps we know *now* how it might be possible to avoid being turned to ice or deformed.

It would be enough to restore to the translation—and to the mind too—the stereotypes, places, *abstract arrangement* of which our gaze had deprived it. For the problem posed to translators can accept only *one* solution: not, of course, by substituting simple abstract words for the clichés of the original text (for the ease and particular nuance of the phrase would thus be lost); nor by translating the cliché word for word (for in doing so one would add to the text a metaphor it had not had before); but rather by making the reader able to *grasp the translation as a cliché* as the original reader, the original listener, must have understood it, and make him immediately *come back* from the image or from the concrete detail, rather than linger over them.

This demands, I know, a certain education on the reader's part, and on the side of the author himself. Perhaps it is not too much to ask of someone, if this effort is *also* one that will allow him to travel back from immediate thought to authentic thought. That is, if we do not want to learn just about the *Iliad,* but about that more secret text that everyone carries within himself. We have recognized, in passing, the rhetorical *treatment.*

We sometimes say, thoughtlessly, that the rules imposed by rhetoricians and grammarians are purely arbitrary, and we do not see in the least to what necessity of thought it is that rhyme or the number of metric feet could answer. But if it is on the contrary the given thought that carries, by the very fact of this *given* and our gaze, all the signs of the arbitrary and the false, we should first of all recognize in rhythm, rhyme, and metric feet this singular value and merit: that by returning to the mind the stereotypes and commonplaces of which our attention had deprived it, they restore it to its original state.

In which the problem is turned upside down, and the Machiavellianism of Rhetoric is justified.

A singular adventure has befallen us: as if the problem we began by posing, far from being resolved, had in some way been turned upside down. It was at first a sort of scandal of reason to us that rhetoric took on its value only by reference to an unconscious mind—an actual one, of course, whose effects we could observe, but one finally that escaped our grasp.

But this mind has not stopped escaping us. Our discovery turned elsewhere: in short, it is not at all because rhetorical thought was abnormal and artificial that we remained powerless to represent it to ourselves, but rather because it was a little too normal and natural—I mean too close to nature and to those original thoughts of which our ideas and our feelings, as soon as we *distinguish* them, are no more than a distorted echo.

I have not said that this discovery was rare, or at all unexpected. All in all, it only justifies the impression that perennially comes to torment us. And what else could the concern signify, common to rhetoricians, for a mind *a little more* spiritual than is ordinary? It was indeed regarding Rhetoric that the paradox of reflection seemed to us *particularly* intolerable. Finally, who does not know from experience that there is more than one poem, and one line, where the eternal, the immediate, the intimate, and what is *common to everyone,* like day and night, space and time, are reflected as in a mirror—one of those mirrors with which the pretty young country girl adorns herself.

KEY TO POETRY

A first version of this text was published anonymously in January 1944, in the inaugural issue of the journal *Message*, entitled "*Sources de la poésie*" (Sources of Poetry). Upon its publication in book form, the title of Paulhan's "Key" grew to the manifesto-like *Key to Poetry: Making It Possible to Distinguish What Is False from What Is True in Any Observation or Doctrine Regarding Rhyme, Rhythm, Verse, the Poet, and Poetry.*

It seems that Paulhan had hoped never to sign this text, going so far as to declare to a friend that "one doesn't sign a theorem or a subtraction." This comment underscores the strange and sometimes contradictory claims to scientificity and mathematical precision that are a driving impulse behind Paulhan's efforts to isolate his "key" and that lead him to cast his various observations in the form of arguments, proofs, and laws—and even to venture the occasional algebraic formula. The text nevertheless appeared under Paulhan's name when it was published by Gallimard in October of the same year, accompanied by the "Observations" that follow. The text is included in the *Œuvres complètes,* volume 2, pp. 241–76.

KEY TO POETRY

Translated by Eric Trudel

ARGUMENT 1

I am not looking to make the slightest poetic discovery, I am looking only for a means of judging every poetic discovery. I do not wish to formulate some new doctrine in poetry; I am looking only for a procedure capable of putting every doctrine to the test. In short, what follows is neither critical nor—obviously—literary. It is strictly logical. And perhaps it is only fair to recall here that studies of this kind have never been considered amusing. Besides, no one has to read them. None of this has been anxiously awaited, and everyone knows that poetry puts up very well with the vague and contradictory opinions that we hold about it.

Here is the most common of places for vagueness and contradiction. We begin, ordinarily, by admitting that there is, at the heart of poetry, a mystery that is strictly unspeakable. Yet we then go on to deal with the particulars of this poetry, by laws or by rules, with the same simplicity we would deal with sulfur, weight, or the weather. But if the mystery is essential to poetry—as was initially alleged—each poetic trait, from rhyme to the spiritual exercise must, on the contrary, bear the mark of this mystery and in some way convey it. There is therefore every likelihood that the laws proposed to us, in spite of looking grammatical or scientific, are false. This is the first point.

Unable to express the poetic mystery, or even reflect on it, I can at least know the elements from which it is made: namely, thought on the one hand and language on the other, ideas and words, meanings and sounds. I can also know the relationship that exists between these elements: it is that of a passage or a conversion of thought into language, such that meaning and sound, idea and word, are interchangeable. This is the second point.

I am imagining now a poetic law that, expressing the particular relationship of sound to meaning and ideas to words, can withstand seeing its terms inverted, without losing either its proofs or its plausibility: that can withstand being reversed. I mean that it henceforth asserts about meaning what it first claimed about words, and about words what it claimed about meaning. It is obvious that such a law, whose formula would be double in this way, would surpass mere plausibility and reach the truth. Indeed, for want of conveying the mystery directly—which is by definition impossible—it would yield to this mystery: it would mime it and show it at work. Hence I can conclude—and this is the last point—that any theory or law of poetry will be accurate inasmuch as it tolerates such a reversal and is careful to cede to the mystery in its dealings with poetry.

The various inquiries, doctrines and aphorisms, commentaries and confessions with which we see poetry afflicted these days give rise to the keenest desire finally to isolate some method or key that will allow us to distinguish true from false. I intend here to forge that key.

1.
IN WHICH POETRY SEEMS TO CONSIST OF TWO PARTS, ONE OF WHICH IS MYSTERIOUS

The common opinion about poetry—even among poets—is curiously divided, as if it consisted of two irreconcilable parts. Here is the first of those parts, and the most obvious one.

If I disregard a certain vertigo and rapture whose nature is vague, I see initially in poetry a constant trait on which doctrines, confessions, and common sense unreservedly agree—the only one suited, therefore, to the foundation of my method.

This trait appears to be simple, obvious, regular, and yet so strange that it would explain the vertigo rather well; it is accessible to the ignorant and the learned alike, and identical for both; it arises at a given point—an object lending itself to scientific inquiry if ever there was one.

With this exception: it escapes our grasp, defeats our reason, exceeds our language. Within us, inconceivable: before our eyes, invisible. We call this trait of poetry its mystery or its secret. Sometimes the critic acknowledges this mystery, and honestly indicates the point at which his analyses cease to be valid and his laws are at fault. At other times he betrays it in spite of himself, and the best proof of this mystery is the arbitrariness or the vanity of the rules he proposes.

And yet who, unless a coward, would resist formulating certitudes like those of physics or geometry? I will not consent to this, all the less so because the laws are as undeniable, from the common sense point of view, as is the mystery itself. All the more so from the specialists' point of view. Such is the second part of common opinion.

Both the romantic and the classical poets, both the surrealist and the rhetorician, acknowledge that there exist in poetry laws that, when obeyed, give their works greatness and their very existence, or that make them pompous and pretentious when ignored. And it is plain to see that some hold these laws to be similar to laws of physics, which are inflexible and apply without our assent: we are only permitted to go along with them or try to dodge them; others compare them to civic or moral laws, which it is in our power to enforce, and which would not exist without us.

There stems from this division of poetry into laws and mystery a difficulty liable to discourage us. For all poetic law, in order to be comprehensive and accurate, ought somehow to include the mystery. But this mystery is elusive. Even if there were a law capable of acknowledging, containing, and making room for it, without being destroyed by it, how could such a law be put into words? How could it be thought?

2.
FURTHER POINTS ON THE MYSTERY: IT IS INCONCEIVABLE BUT BANAL; OBSCURE BUT DAZZLING

By *law* I mean, in the most ordinary but also the most rigorous sense, the regularly occurring relation we may observe or produce between two facts. When an apple is ripe and comes off the tree, it falls to the ground. If I drop a stone and a wad of cotton into the void, they fall at equal speed. But the mystery is more difficult. We must beware certain foreign ideas associated with it, and liable to lead to its betrayal.

We commonly associate a vague hope with the idea of mystery. It is that this mystery must be somehow reducible to a problem, one that cannot fail to be solved one day, and the mystery to become clear. But I must also contend that the mystery, conversely, will nonetheless remain *inconceivable,* even if *intelligible* and present in us and for us. In such a way that the various clear ideas we can have of it are all unfaithful, as if indifferent in their inaccuracy. This is the first point. It amounts simply to saying that the mystery is mysterious. Here is the second point:

Mystery is often associated with the idea of rarity. Because mystery remains opaque to our intelligence, we conclude that it is exceptional (as if it were extraordinary for us to be baffled!). Yet it is obvious that the mystery we are dealing with here, quite to the contrary, is banal and arises at the slightest provocation. Clearly it is impossible to consider, to hold, to have; but for anyone who seeks not to have it, but to *be* it, it is the easiest thing there is. It is enough to read a poem. It is enough to expect to read a poem. It is enough, if you will, to be in the mood for a poem. In short, given certain conditions, the mystery comes perfectly naturally. It is no more a problem (which could be solved) than it is a miracle (which would elude natural laws); rather it is itself regular, and prepared to be law.

Here is the final point: common sense readily believes that there is something like a dark radiance surrounding a mystery, a contagiousness of darkness—and that everything that touches the mystery becomes, like it, inconceivable. Here again, it is quite obviously the opposite that takes place. One does not write a poem about the forest to lose sight of the forest; one does not read a love sonnet to be finished with love. Poetry does not conceal the rocks and passions of which it speaks. On the contrary, it shows them to us and seems even to reveal them, as if they had remained obscure to us until that moment. In a word, the mystery sheds light all around. (And perhaps there is no light that does not also suppose some mystery.)

3. THE ELEMENTS OF THE MYSTERY ARE THOSE OF ALL EXPRESSION: SIGN AND MEANING

Let us better specify a point: poetry is not, in our everyday experience, a monster unrelated to anything. We are quick to call *poetic* those moments when all of nature seems to befriend us, as if entering into a conversation: a lake at dawn, a storm, a sunset. We go so far as to say (a bit foolishly) that "there is more poetry in a prairie at dusk than in all our books of poems." And in between the poem and the prairie, all the things one can think of. There are letters and prayers, novels and essays, even cries, laughter, or tears that are poetic. In sum, for poetry to exist, it is necessary—but it seems to be sufficient—that there be communication, conversation, some intercourse.

Which explains why we are able to grasp of this poetry (and hence of the very mystery it holds), if not its nature, then the elements that are sufficient to it, and that are all that poetry uses. They are the elements of any expression. Now, these elements, at least, are familiar to me. I am able to tell one from another, I can name them. On the one hand, there are the letter and the sign, breath, sound, all of them things external to us, material, and seemingly offered to our senses: to sight, to hearing, to touch. On the other hand, there are significations with which these are associated: ideas, wishes, feelings, all of them things known to us through intimate experience, escaping both our senses and any quantification. In short, poetry is as diverse—and of the same sort of diversity—as the objects it presents to us: it has its matter and its spirit, its body and its soul, its forests and its passions.

I am only stating the obvious. It must, however, be said, in a domain where obviousness is not without its difficulties. It may well be that there are constant relationships between this matter and this spirit, between this word and this thought, given by nature, and other than those laid down by grammar or the dictionary. I do not see anything shocking in this. Tracking them down is no doubt a matter of being patient, rigorous, and meticulous. However, I also know that poetry has its mystery. Granted. I must therefore admit that there exists a mode of joining or of combining these clear elements, such that their combination is intelligible to us, and yet still exceeds what our mind can grasp: perfectly inconceivable. I will not consider myself satisfied until I have determined this relation. It will be, in a way, our first test. And there is more: I know that there must exist, between mystery and the law, a relationship such that the law becomes meaningful only on mystery's terms. This is poetry's other paradox.

4.
IN WHICH THE POETS' OBSERVATIONS CONFLICT: THE LETTER AGAINST SPIRIT

I have no choice but to begin by interrogating the poets. They are my first witnesses. Hazardous witnesses, to be sure, and partial—each one haunted by the idea that his poetry must be the best (otherwise, why would they even venture being poets?) and busy with making his doctrine work toward this poetry's perfection. That is not all: each of them wants his doctrine to demonstrate this perfection. All are naturally tendentious, not a little biased. It would be unfair to demand of them the patience, the rigor, and the detachment we require from a scholar, or even a connoisseur. In any case, they are in the thick of poetry like Eskimos in the cold. They live it, breathe it, swim in it. What is more, the descriptions they give, and the laws they claim to reveal, exhibit certain constant features: the same appearance, the same content. Even the conflict between them is consistent and seems regulated by law: this is the first thing that strikes me.

Let me make something clear: I do not choose between poets. No more do I choose between observers or doctrinarians of poetry. (Rather, I tend to see in their differences an effect of the mystery I am trying to circumscribe: a mystery is what everyone is free to understand in his own way.) I acknowledge Shelley with Rimbaud, Victor Hugo as well as Horace, Poe and Apollinaire alike. Yet their explanations and doctrines share a singular trait: each of them is ingenious, probable—and what is more, because they are also poets—proven by facts. But not so much so that the opposite explanation does not also remain probable—and no less proven.

For Apollinaire and Novalis make language, in poetry, proceed from an inspiration. But Poe and Valéry derive inspiration from a language. The latter see in material permutations the origin of all poetic spirit; the former see in their spiritual exercise the very reason for the letter and for rhythm. The revelation, says one, produces its own words and own form. Yet the other says: the form and the words cause the revelation. "Poetry," says Boccaccio, "is Theology." "Little more than word games and riddles," answers Malherbe. "The poet is the pope," says Victor Hugo. "At best a chess player," replies Banville. "He is a prophet," "He is a goldsmith," "He sings," "He calculates." Hence we see every treatise on poetry turn into metaphysics or prosody. Take your pick.

So all poets accept in common that there exist poetic laws; I mean by this a relation of cause and effect between elements of expression. It is merely that some poets make the form proceed from the content, others, the content from the form.

This is ordinarily accompanied by a certain disdain for consequence, and great esteem for the cause. "Inspiration comes from the reader," say some. But others: "Let us leave rules to the helpless." Here we see more clearly still that we are dealing not with scholars, but with technicians, practical people whose express aim is to obtain a certain effect: the poetic effect, precisely.

5. IN WHICH POETIC DOCTRINES ARE IN AGREEMENT: PROCESSES OR FUNCTIONS

In moving from one explanation to another, we recognized the opposition of the two great doctrines or two *perspectives* between which the intellectual realm is divided: with some holding that thought comes from form and matter, others that form is born of thought. This is the whole metaphysical difference between materialists and idealists; the whole political difference between fascists and democrats, and between traditionalists and revolutionaries. It is the whole debate between the letter and spirit. Thus, in a domain closer to our own—if not in fact the same—the name is sometimes explained by the thing. (How well *shroud,* we say, renders the shroud! How this name seems called forth by the object.) But sometimes the thing is explained by the name. (It is not unintentional that *weasels* [les belettes] are called *pretty little things* [petites belles] in thirty languages. It is in hopes of getting them, through this flattering name, to behave in a gentler fashion.) Besides, they move effortlessly from one kind of explanation to another: this one, a democrat in politics, is a materialist when it comes to philosophy. This one, a classicist in poetry, is a democrat in politics. And many a critic will speak by turns, according to the occasion, the language of the rhetorician or that of the terrorist.[1] So freely does our mind move in its contradiction.

But our doctrinarians are attempting to be more rigorous. The subject they deal with—expression—seems more established, more clearly delimited, and to lend itself more readily to experience than do those great realms of the soul or of society, whose consequences escape us. (One suspects that the key, once discovered, would also be valid for many domains other than literature or poetry.)

However, the laws before us exhibit, alongside this general tendency to be in direct opposition, several common features. Here is the most readily apparent: it is not to language *in general* that the rhetoricians attribute a singular power, nor do the terrorists to thought; rather it is in every case assigned to *functions,* as mathematics says; to *concentrations* or *granulations,* as physics says; to *structures* of words or of thoughts, as philosophy says—all precise processes or combinations whose formulae can be determined, in such a way that there follows, for a new set of language or of thought, some new property that was not found in the elements.

Hence the rhetorician does not advise the poet to trust in naked words, but rather in a patient effort that gathers these words and combines them according to the laws of rhyme or rhythm, antithesis or metaphor, hyperbole or synecdoche. Nor does the terrorist advise him to trust in thought alone, as it comes to us, haphazardly, but in the treatment of this thought by enthusiasm or purity, by the refusal of reason, or of morals, or of logic, by the isolation of the spontaneous flow of the soul. All are processes or permutations by which the most contradictory doctrines are each made effective, and the laws are justified. It sometimes happens that the same treatment is suggested in both registers: this is the case, for instance, with metaphor. But as a result the opposition is only more palpable, the absurdity more obvious.

As ingenious as the treatment may be, the fact remains that there is no reflection or law here that can be considered unironically, because we could just as well have conducted the opposite reflection. Hence poetry's very existence becomes curiously questionable, as if continually deferred.

6.
IN WHICH THE MYSTERY IS EXPRESSED INSTEAD OF THOUGHT

More often than not, poets and critics get out of this through suspicion or disdain. "He's not telling the whole truth, he's joking, he's bluffing, he's keeping secrets." This is deep down what Poe thinks of Shelley, what Du Bos says of Valéry and Valéry of Apollinaire. It is quite natural for them to think this. But if we are not to treat half the poets with contempt, we are denied this nature and this door is closed to us. This leaves us with the opposite course: which is to take them all *equally* seriously. It is easy to see why such a course would be plausible, even if our research had not forced us to adopt it.

For there is one trait that strikes us as these reflections draw to a close: it is that poetry, contrary to the explanations of it that are given, is obviously simple: free and bare, and not hindered by any theory. When doctrinarians and critics have used up all their reasons, naive poetry rises up and takes flight. We are astonished to see it so fresh—so different from reasons. To be sure, the reflections carried out by Baudelaire and Shelley, Lamartine and Mallarmé, have nothing in common—not even the language they use. And yet their works are similar in effect, more so than we might have expected on the basis of their doctrine. (Otherwise, would we even be speaking of poetry?) This poet, who seeks nothing but spiritual adventure and revelation, does not write *all that differently* from the other one who talks only of measure and craft. More than one of Poe's verses might have been written by Shelley. More than one of Verlaine's verses by Apollinaire.

Let us dream of loosely analogous mysteries. I imagine that Mr. Piccard flies off into the stratosphere at exactly five o'clock, whereas Mr. Halphen plunges toward the center of the earth. If it happens that Mr. Piccard runs into Mr. Halphen at six o'clock, I will have no choice but to suppose that, in the meantime, one or the other of them—if not both—has deviated a little from his initial trajectory. Either that, or that there is in the nature of the sky and of the earth something that they had not anticipated. It is as if, in poetry too, there were a moment when every poet finds himself obliged to neglect his particular choice in order to follow the opposite one, and in doing so repudiates his first commitment. It is at this moment that the singer's hopes add up, and the calculator starts singing: Rimbaud becomes Boileau, without admitting it; and Valéry becomes Novalis in silence. (As if poets differed only in virtue of that part of their poetry they keep hidden. The classical poet, secretly a romantic; the surrealist, a rhetorician without saying so.) But more precisely—let me return to my method.

We have seen that there was one constant trait to poetry: it is the routine inadequacy that every doctrine or reason betrays in dealing with it. As if the various clear ideas we were able to form of poetry were all equally faulty and thus were characterized, beneath their apparent diversity, by their sameness. In a word, it comes down to the same thing whether one makes use, in poetry, of inspiration or industry, dream or calculation. It makes no difference whether one treats it, essentially, as words (from which would arise emotion) or as thoughts (from which would proceed words and phrases).

If I try less to explain this trait, or even to understand it, than to express it—to formulate it—I arrive at the following: that in poetry words and thoughts happen to be *indifferent.*

7.
IN WHICH OUR DISCOVERY IS PUT TO THE TEST

That this trait peculiar to poetry escapes the grasp of poets (and ourselves) is no cause for surprise, if this is the trait that our mind is by nature incapable of conceiving. Here, common sense and the philosophers agree. This one endlessly repeats, "A penny is a penny. When it is night, it is not day. A door is either open or closed." The others, more gravely, speak of the principle of identity, of contradiction, of the excluded third term: "What is, they say (in a rather enigmatic fashion), is." Or else: "What is not true is false." Or, if we prefer, "What is word is not thought; and what is thought is not word." And maybe we ought to reply to common sense, to the philosophers—if this principle is indeed the one necessarily governing each step of our mind—how strange it is that this mind nevertheless knows how to isolate it, to consider it, how strange indeed that we would even be invited to respect it, as if there existed some other state that contrasted with it and made it possible for us to distinguish this one. But were we not also led to recognize the existence of this other state as we followed some unexpected path? Its existence, and this quality that seems specific to it: the fact that it cannot be conceived. As if it occupied, while it is occurring, the totality of a mind from which not the slightest part could be withdrawn to observe it. Such that our tormented thought, sensing its presence but incapable of grasping it, is here reduced to allusions and myths: the void, the absurd, the blank page, universal language, the revelations of etymology, the golden language in which the Word is accessible to our senses and words merge with the thing itself. Reduced to jokes and formulas: "Any speech being idea . . . form and content are one and the same . . . it's funny but when the form is new, so is the content. . . . In order to renew the idea, it is necessary to innovate in style . . ."[2] and all the other obvious maxims that are listened to—admired, even—although it is perfectly vain and absurd, according to them, to try to admit that matter is spirit, that outside is inside, that the self and the other merge and become one. In short, we can say these things, but not think them.

That was, remember, our first test: it adds nothing to our confusion. Incidentally, we could have made the same discovery with less effort: it was enough, simply, to ask ourselves what kind of relationship there could be between word and idea, such that it escapes from view and produces the mystery. I can see only one: it is that the word becomes idea and the idea becomes word, so much so that—because each term in the relationship loses the particular features that define it—the relationship cannot even be imagined.

There is an easy answer to the objection that we cannot take an inconceivable event into account in our calculations. It is that, this being the case, we ought to approach it any way we can, and let the verbal formulation go forward even if our thought does not! Besides, because everything dictates that we expect a mystery, it would be odd to abandon our inquiry at the moment it brings us just what we were looking for. The mathematician and the physicist do not hesitate to use, in the course of their reasoning (though they avoid dwelling on them), terms that are, for that matter, just as inconceivable: imaginary numbers, quantum of action, space-time or movement-figure (the latter so close to our idea-word). I do not lay claim to greater rigor than theirs. But I do lay claim to the same rigor.

8.
OF A KEY MADE OF LANGUAGE, OR THE FORMULA OF A MODEL LAW

I am looking for a key that will enable me to distinguish, among the laws of poetry currently in use, true from false, exact from inexact. Therefore, and to begin with, I welcome these laws as they are given to me, with their accidents and their constants: their condition. This condition is so precise that I can draw up its formula.

If I designate words and ideas by a b c, α β γ —a b c being words if α β γ are ideas, and vice versa—but the sets or functions organizing these words and ideas by F and F', I arrive in fact at a formula for these laws. This formula is unique, whatever the poetic event being considered—image, commonplacc, antithesis—such that:

From F (a b c) it follows that F' (α β γ)

where it is simply understood that a b c are words for classicists and rhetoricians, and α β γ ideas. But for romantic poets and terrorists, a b c are, on the contrary, ideas and α β γ words.

Meanwhile, I was also able to determine the formula of the mystery—even though I had given up, once and for all, the hope of thinking it. Because the cause of mystery is the identity of words and thoughts, it would be:

$$a = \alpha \; b = \beta \; c = \gamma$$

or:

$$a \, b \, c = \alpha \, \beta \, \gamma$$

This being so, there is nothing more to prevent me, if I bring the two formulas together, from expressing the key I am looking for.

Any law of poetry must, by definition, pass two kinds of test. The first one is common to all scientific laws. Whether it is verified by experience, whether it is capable of being dealt with by theorems of transfer, residue, concordance, and deviation, are questions I need not ask here; they are matters of patience and rigor. But the second test, which interests me, is peculiar to a poetic law: it is a matter of knowing whether this law remains valid *in spite of* the mystery and the transmutation of its elements; if it will resist this mystery and (so to speak) absorb the obstacle. But I do not know if such laws exist. I do not know—if indeed they exist—if they are conceivable. For the moment, this is of no concern to me. But I see clearly what requirement they would need to meet in order to exist. They would need to remain identical, unchanged—I mean *establishing,* from a given function F to another F', the *same* causal relationship—*whatever the order of the elements* that fall into these sets or functions: either that ideas are the cause, and words the effect; or that the words on the contrary are the cause, and the ideas the consequence. Thus for any law I arrive at the double formula:

From F (a b c) it follows that F' (α β γ)
From F (α β γ) it follows that F' (a b c)

The only thing I have left to do is to apply this formula to the current laws, and find them exact if they yield to it, false if they fail.

At this point, I can ask myself if I have found something even better than a formula—something that might allow me to assess with certainty the truth or falseness of every law. But how would it be possible to go further, and conceive the law (if it is true) in its simplicity, in what makes *a single law* valid for *a single* given trait of poetry? First of all, I would have to conceive, if only for an instant, that words and ideas are one and the same thing—or at least think, taking the mystery as a point of departure, about the particulars of the law and its various applications. I would have to admit, for example, that every image is a function of words, but, at the same time, a group of thoughts. . . . Let us leave this aside. And, by the way, it would have been possible for me to follow a different path.

9.
OF A KEY MADE OF THOUGHT, OR THE MEANING OF A MODEL LAW

If I leave aside any formula, and look for what the *meaning* of an exact law of poetry would be, here is what I find.

The problem is to know under what conditions the law, along with the mystery included within it, would be accessible to us. We may note first of all that this mystery is not necessarily a source of obscurity. We have seen, on the contrary, what clarity—elevated to a sense of revelation—its presence gave to the objects of the poem. If I could manage to understand, thanks to the law, the elements of poetry according to this same mystery, ideas and words would become just as clear to me as this other sort of matter and these other thoughts are in the poem: stones and trees, fears and passions. Of course, it would not amount to much for this law to be clear if it remained incommunicable. Yet I know that the mystery can be neither said nor thought directly.

It would therefore be necessary for the mystery to be implied in the law. This is still not enough to stop us. It is by no means exceptional, in fact it is a rule that any expression, aside from what it says openly, contains a secret part—secret, but no less there. The simplest question, "What is going on?" or "What have you got?" means, depending on the circumstances (is the person asking a doctor, a friend, a financier, a customs officer?): "what is worrying you? . . ." or "what is ailing you? . . ." or "what do you own? . . ." or "have you anything to declare?" and so on.[3] Similarly, there is no theorem or law of physics that does not imply twenty unspoken definitions: an entire other order, akin to a division of the world. There exists in any sentence a secret space likely to host a mystery.

A difficulty, however, remains: the mathematician—or the friend, or the doctor—is ready to think and say in detail, if necessary, what he was not saying a moment ago. The same cannot be true of an inconceivable mystery.

Let us be careful here. As inconceivable as it is, the mystery is not, for all that, less intelligible. Certainly it is of such a nature that we cannot hope to comprehend it. But why not realize it, trigger it, and in the end, *be* it? We commonly say of the concerns, reflections, and fears hidden from us by propriety and taboos, by the caution of our conversation, that they are *unconscious.* This is a fortuitous or accidental *unconscious,* one that the psychologist's analysis brings to light—and that another society, other customs could make conscious. But when it comes to the mystery, it seems that we are dealing on the contrary with a necessary or a *natural unconscious*—another state of reflection, another disposition of the mind—such that no human effort can shed light on it. Yet it is the most consistent and most normal there is, the easiest to provoke.

I may now extract the key made of meaning that I need.

I am looking for a law that would be partly made of mystery. More precisely: a law that will necessarily induce this secret way of seeing, this thought that is so elusive, yet so easily triggered by the slightest provocation (to which we have given the name *mystery*). Such that this mystery, making up its tacit part, will flood the law with its light.

For that purpose, it is enough for me to imagine a reversible law, capable of double expression, where words tolerate substitution for ideas, and ideas for words—*sets or functions remaining identical*—without the law losing any of its precision: equally verifiable in one form or the other, such that language and thought are revealed to be strictly indifferent terms. So much so that, in the end, the entire law needs to be thought in its particulars on the basis of this indifference.

In short, the same sort of law whose formula I established by following another path.

Let the reader be kind enough to apply this key to the commentaries, asides, themes, and doctrines prevailing in poetry. I am confident that he will be led to more than one remark or discovery that may disappoint him at first, but will gratify him afterward.

ARGUMENT 2

"That hollow formula (someone will say) hasn't got us very far if no law can be found to comply with it. You stop at the point where things should get started."

The objection continues: "Besides, this is not how a science comes about or progresses. On the contrary. The scientist, be it Descartes or Newton, first makes his discovery, and only afterwards does he ask himself what he could have done to make it."

More specifically: "What is a valid method, after all, if not a first discovery that the discoverer, in order to extend it—to duplicate it—sums up and brings to the level of an abstraction?"

And finally: "But I look in vain for your discovery. Moreover, your intention itself was absurd. One can only judge a poetic doctrine by comparing it to what is already known, for a fact, about poetry."

It is true enough that I did not try to make any personal discovery. I simply assumed—it was not too bold of me—that the discovery had already been made, and that it was unlikely that the poets who have dealt with poetry have been, in general, absolutely wrong. I had this proof: their work itself, and their poems. I took seriously the most ordinary of the prevailing opinions about poetry: that form cannot be distinguished from content. In short, I started by assuming that the matter had been solved. And, oddly, I was rewarded for my confidence.

What in fact did I discover as I persevered, on the one hand, on the side of pure language, until now limited to a formula, to reach a proposition eluding the strictest language at our disposal, mathematics (hence more rigorous than rigor itself), by virtue of the rigorous ambiguity of its terms (a b c being thoughts if α β γ are words; but words if α β γ are thoughts); and as I persevered, on the other hand, on the side of pure thought, until I came to consider as an idea the very thing that is present to the mind but cannot be considered by it, that eludes all science of psychology, being inconceivable if not intelligible? What did I discover as I thus pursued, stubbornly, here my equations and there my thoughts, if not—at the end of these two parallel paths between which no communication or passage is even imaginable—exactly the same requirement and the same type of law? There was nothing in my formula that allowed me to hope that it could be thought; quite the contrary, and yet I thought it. Neither was there anything in my key made of thought (had I discovered it first) that led me to believe it could be reduced to language; and yet I expressed it. I did not formulate anything that I did not think, or imagine anything that did not get expressed elsewhere. In such a way that ideas and words in the end appear to be, to me too, within the limits of this specific analysis, indifferent.

I said before, it is true, that my argument was strictly logical. And, as one sees in other adventures, the outcome has simply exceeded my argu-

ment. Logical, yes, and something more, which I have no choice but to call poetic.

Let us push the objection further. What is a method, you said, if not first a discovery then brought to abstraction? Undeniably. But in that case, what is a discovery if not a method that one makes concrete and, precisely, experiences? Now, it turned out that my key was also my experience: and I discovered more than a hollow formula. In the very experience I discovered a first law yielding to the key, one that fulfills it and authenticates it. A law that is, like the key, double, if it maintains both that words must take the place of meaning, and meaning of words. I have proposed nothing that I have not myself been through. It is not much to make a discovery: I was the very discovery I was making. So that it is enough, in the end, if I want to verify my formula, to apply it to the reasoning that allowed me to invent it.

I spoke of a poetic event. But there are other terms that would not be less exact. If the experience (together with the mystery it supposes) can be repeated at will, we readily see that it is likely to transform the very nature of a Rhetoric—hereafter based not on external tricks, but on a conviction born of an interior release. And likely to transform the nature of a Critique that in the future will be based not on rules and measures, but on a strict participation or, if you prefer, on a sharing of poetry's secret: in short, a Critique in full knowledge of the facts.

"If this is the case (someone will say again), it is therefore in keeping with the same mystery, once it has been established (espoused as well as understood, triggered and grasped in a single movement), that you should now be able to understand the most trifling feature of your investigation, the least little detail of the key: rhyme, image, and the rest—as the poet understands stones or passions."

I believe so. And yet, it is no longer my task to answer here, but my reader's (yes, I am talking to you), if you have had the extraordinary patience to follow me, and to find yourself suddenly transformed.

OBSERVATIONS

a) The linguists at fault[4]

The reader may have been tempted previously to object that, in dealing with laws and rules, we should have turned first to scientists (in fact, to linguists) rather than to poets and critics. For the linguist confronts language events in all innocence, with the sole concern of understanding them and grouping them by laws, without the least desire to use them.

That is true. Yet, at least if our conclusions are correct and our law is well founded, this very disinterest must fail the linguist more than it serves him. What we have discovered is not that poetry should be observed without bias. Far from it. Instead, we found that it was advisable to mix and match the different current prejudices among poets regarding poetry.

First, let us be precise. It is out of the question to seek the advice of the phoneticians, who curiously decide in advance to take into consideration, of all the facts they observe, only sounds and noises, syllables and letters. Neither should we turn to semanticists, who are preoccupied with ideas and meanings, yet decide, conversely, to pay no attention to the materiality of words. If both phoneticians and semanticists succeed in establishing laws, it is on the condition that they subtract from language one of the two elements whose union constitutes it.

There remains a domain of linguistics that was late to develop and is still shaky: stylistics. Among its practitioners I see only two who have taken up the precise revelation of constant relationships and laws between meanings and words: Ferdinand de Saussure, in the *Cours de linguistique générale,* and his disciple Charles Bally, in the *Stylistique française.*[5]

The project of observing words in their relationship to thoughts obviously implies that one is already in possession of a method capable of isolating and classifying these words on the one hand, and, on the other, these thoughts. I do not know if such a method exists; it seems unlikely when we consider how elusive, uncertain, and contradictory Saussure's and Bally's conception of language is. I will underline some of their contradictions.

Saussure writes that thought, if we set aside its expression, "is only a shapeless and indistinct mass, where nothing is delimited."[6] But Bally sets for stylistics the task of "delimiting the events of language until they correspond to indivisible units of thought."[7] Thus, it is sometimes maintained that thought is naturally chaotic, and at other times that it is naturally organized.

"It is rare," Bally remarks, "for language to offer us side by side three terms of comparison: neutral term, laudatory term (*freedom*), pejorative term (*licentiousness*) . . . because the mind is too lazy to think three things at once."[8] However, Saussure observes that "the syntagma *let's walk* supposes some linguistic association, on the one hand, with the set *walk* (singular imperative), *walk* (plural imperative) . . . and, on the other, with the set *let's climb, let's eat. . . .*" He adds: "When someone says: *let's walk,* he thinks unconsciously of these diverse sets of associations."[9] And Bally: "Our mind is active to the point of calling up, along with a word, the varied synonyms and antonyms of this word."[10] Thus it is sometimes maintained that the mind is naturally lazy, sometimes that it is naturally active.

Bally holds our mind to be incapable of spontaneous abstraction. Indeed, we cannot "extract a concept from any contact with concrete reality."[11] Neither do we manage to "define pure notions without points of comparison drawn from the external world."[12] However, Bally asserts elsewhere that the mind "realizes in language its preestablished abstract concepts."[13] Against grammatical rules—for instance, the rule stating that *quoique* (although) must be followed by the subjunctive—he argues the following: "It is much more important to know that one is dealing here with an abstract notion, restriction, and that this notion is composed, among other possible realizations, of a syntactic mould: *quoique,* followed by the subjunctive."[14] Thus, it is claimed in one instance that the units of our mind are naturally abstract, and in another, that they are naturally concrete.

Bally also asserts that the mind "can only think things in connection with other, related things."[15] Yet he adds, a little further, that "any unit of thought is strictly limited by other units of thought."[16] And so on and so forth, I could quote endlessly. It is easy to see the cause of these essential contradictions, and of the specific contradictions they impose in turn, without end.

When Bally concludes, from the absence of three terms of comparison, that "our mind is too lazy to think three things at once," or when he writes about those sentences in which a single word is repeated ("No, no, no, never!"): "One cause of repetition is the rush of effects accompanying thought: the emotional impulses have repercussions on expression, and language tends to repeat thought as many times as there are pulsations."[17] (This is like saying, no less cogently, that opium puts you to sleep because it has a soporific property.) It is only too clear that he does not offer us a new observation, distinct from the first. He is merely translating into psychological terms the linguistic event he observed. Language, here, is far from being the sign of thought, and rather is it thought that, for the linguist, is a way of translating language. Thought is a sign of this language.

But, conversely, Bally writes, for instance, "the Latin term *lupus* represents two very different words, when we read it at the head of an dictionary entry, or when we read it in Virgil's Eclogue: *Triste lupus stabulis*"[18] or: "the word *Walk!* is not irreducible to smaller elements. For the spontaneous associations that give it its meaning (*Will you walk? Do you want to walk? You, walk! Walk, Paul! I want you to walk,* etc.) show that this word not only expresses the idea of walking, but also the notions of the second-person pronoun and of the imperative mood"[19] (and all these other observations that are at the root of stylistics). It is obvious that he is merely translating into the language of linguistics the ideas he thinks he is observing. In short, the specialists in stylistics—though their sole concern is obviously to submit to facts—strangely begin by getting these facts mixed up, and sometimes deal with thought as if it were language, and at other times deal with language as if it were thought.[20] There follow the contradictions we have already noted. Basically we recognize, in a rudimentary form, exactly the same flaw that caused poets and critics at times to consider words as a simple manifestation and consequence of thought, and at other times to consider thought the result of words. From this we ought to draw one more inference: it is that the same flaw could very well have the same cause. This is another reason, which should have been mentioned before, not to turn to linguists first: that they have never shown much concern for poetry, other than for the influence it sometimes exerts over everyday language. They see it as a kind of individual and unpredictable invention, intended for the reader's sensibility more than for his intelligence, thus an invention that escapes their grasp on two counts.

Yes, we might have mentioned this reason. And in a sense it is unfortunate we did not. For it is too late to do it, now that the opposite proof has been, as it were, produced. What we have discovered is that poetry in no way avoids the condition of everyday language. It is exactly the opposite. If the strict and simple observers of language, despite their painstaking efforts, are the victims of the same confusion, and fall into the same trap awaiting the doctrinarians of poetry, if they are all overcome by the event, disappointed, and, if I may say so, conned by it *in the very same way,* this means that the same event that makes poetry was already at work in the simplest expression. It is simply that poetry gives it more relief and more gravity, shows it at work in full light. In short, not even the simplest language can be understood without some mystery. So that there would be great wisdom, despite the apparent paradox of it, in the decision of phoneticians and semanticists—that it to say, the decision, with very few exceptions, of linguists as a whole—to strip this language of one of the two elements whose union constitutes it before trying to grasp it through their simple laws. For the union of these elements, being precisely mysterious in nature, lends itself only to the kind of law whose model we drew up earlier, whose prime example we gave at the same time.

b) The Quarrel of the Image[21]

We have had the opportunity to note that poetry puts up very well with the vague and contradictory opinions (we also say: generous) that we hold about it. But this is rather an understatement, as we now suspect. Poetry needs these opinions. It calls for them and requests them as soon as it wishes to be expressed or even thought.

I will give a fresh example of this, more precise and, if I may say so, better localized than those we have seen thus far. It may have seemed, a moment ago, that I was digging up an overly abstract and philosophical quarrel between idealists and materialists—and an antiquated one at that, seeing that more than one metaphysician thinks he has got beyond it. To this, I could answer that I did not go in search of this quarrel; rather, it found me—the philosophers themselves are, on this issue, less stubbornly metaphysical than common sense, this common sense whose reasoning I had to observe and follow so patiently. I am not looking here to create some new metaphysics, more decisive than the previous one. That is not at all my concern. I am simply trying to force some coherence on a popular metaphysics, one that routinely offers itself together with language and the very play of meaning—all the more so with poetry: an *inevitable* metaphysics. That said, I still have to prove that a positive-looking opposition, seemingly protected against any metaphysical irruption, would have served my argument just as well.

Paul Souday, Edmond Jaloux, André Breton, Jean Prévost, and the other critics who have dealt with the works of the surrealists are all in agreement about their nature. The thought expressed in them only lends itself, according to Edmond Jaloux and André Breton, to "the production of the most beautiful images."[22] Paul Souday and Jean Prévost note, for their part, that "the surrealists put the entire art of writing into the image."[23] Criticism thus seems to be on solid ground, where we could expect it to offer a sound description and judgment of the work it is examining. Surrealism as well, because of the clarity and monotony of its features, seems to call for this judgment, this description:

> The least hem of the breezes, there where the pheasant of the moon flees and dies.
> The park stretched its blond hands over the magic fountain.
> On the bridge the dew with the head of a tabby cat lulls itself to sleep.[24]

Even if it should happen that the critics differ, how can we not suppose that the disparity between them, emerging on a precise and clearly defined ground, will be easily, if not resolved, then at least exactly interpreted and situated?

It turns out that this disparity is one of the most difficult we can find.

Indeed, the agreement lasts for only this fleeting moment that they are speaking of *images*. Jean Prévost condemns these images and all of surrealism along with them. André Breton admires and praises them. It is not about any of their particular qualities, nor about some accidental feature, peculiar to surrealism. No, it is about their essential character, about the very thing that makes them images. It is enough for them to be images, and Breton puts all authentic activity of the mind within their realm:

> All these images seem to attest to the fact that the mind is ripe for something more than the benign joys it allows itself in general. This is the only way it has of turning to its own advantage the ideal quantity of events with which it is entrusted.[25]

Jean Prévost, however, sees in them:

> A mediocre game, which they curiously abuse. . . .

He adds:

> A work survives by the just relationship between feeling and expression, not because of images.

But here is the surprising thing: Jean Prévost and André Breton start with the same critical opinion and apply the same principles. Indeed, Breton writes:

> Experience paces back and forth in a cage from which it is more and more difficult to make it emerge . . . how could the mind find itself at ease within the limits in which . . . almost all book imprison it?[26]

And Jean Prévost:

> The real discoveries about ourselves, about the universe and everything else, far from having been made already, are far from our even thinking them possible—we can't even desire them or conceive of them.

What matters here is nothing but novelty or originality. We need only put a little pressure on Breton and Prévost and they will reveal the meaning and reason of this originality. To emerge from the cage where "experience paces back and forth," we need, says Breton, "to attack language, which is the worst convention, before anything." Or else "we shouldn't stop putting words to shame." We even ought to

> turn them away from their ability to signify, thus rendering their betrayal impossible.

Jean Prévost, for his part, accuses most of modern literature of being nothing more than "printed matter built on other printed matter." Or else, he writes:

> The human substance contained in a literary work is what makes it valuable. As for the modes of expression, they vary according to circumstances. A literary device is never worth anything in itself. . . . No stylistic form is essential.

There is nothing surprising in these declarations. They are prevalent in our days, and there are few critical opinions in which they do not appear, at least allusively. Breton and Prévost are only repeating with greater conviction what had already been suggested by Apollinaire or Novalis, Rimbaud, Victor Hugo, in short, by the faction of the Romantics and the Terrorists. Authentic poetry, with its laws, is in their opinion one that moves from thought to language, and not from language to thought.

It is therefore all the more surprising that, because they agree to see in a given work the exclusive presence of images—thus agreeing both on the principle of their judgment and on the particular fact to which it is applied—they can differ so completely in their application. But we ought to examine their reasoning more closely.

After noting that the surrealists put the entire art of writing into the image, Jean Prévost adds how easy it is, hence, to understand surrealism's rhetoric:

> Take a simple and conventional object; refer to it with an extravagant metaphor or at least one that is distant enough; readers will be astounded to find their hat or their pipe hidden under your images.

Jean Prévost goes on to give an example and writes, instead of *newspaper:*

> crushed oak, blackened with the perverse ink of the world. . . .[27]

Instead of *boredom:*

> to me, the shadow gauging and sweeping my days away seems, at times, to be swallowed by the sand. . . .

But André Breton, for his part, writes:

> It is true of surrealist images as it is of opium images that man does not evoke them; rather they come to him spontaneously, despotically. He cannot chase them away. . . . First the mind becomes convinced of the supreme reality of these images. It soon realizes that they increase its knowledge. Images appear, in its dizzying race, like the only guideposts of the mind.[28]

Breton goes on to say that the best and most authentic surrealist images are those that we are not at all capable of "translating into practical language," for instance:

> In the forest aflame the lions were fresh.
> On the bridge the dew with the head of a tabby cat lulls itself to sleep.

Or:

> In the school's chalk there is a sewing machine; little children shake their curls of silver paper.[29]

Thus we realize that Breton and Prévost designate by the same name the two most different things there are: one calls *image* the sentence (preferably mysterious and bizarre) through which a writer translates a given object and beneath which he dissimulates it. The other designates, with this same word, the very object and the original event that we can only translate—in a more or less clumsy fashion—into everyday language. The presence in a work of this same event: *the image* is, for one of them, the undeniable sign and proof that the writer started with words. He sees this writer as working backward. He writes:

> Is the image more praiseworthy than another figure of style, than periphrasis for instance?
>
> There is, in our days, a strange, excessive use of this figure of style. It goes without saying that the reign of the antithesis would be just as tiresome.

Yet this same presence appears to the other as a sign of supreme authenticity and the proof that the writer, disregarding all language, trusted only his "unforgiving" imagination:

> It is wrong to claim that the mind has grasped the connection of two opposing realities. I reject the idea that images can offer the least premeditation. . . .[30]

Thus the same standard that leads Prévost to condemn surrealist images compels Breton to praise them. Images, says the one, are loathsome because they are nothing more than puns, and the author bows to language in using them. Images are admirable, says the other, because they attest to the fact that the writer has freed himself of language once and for all. As for Souday, who writes:

> The poets endowed with ideas or imagination long ago discovered devices at least as worthy as those of the surrealists.[31]

He employs the same reasoning as Prévost, while Jaloux sides with Breton:

> The image . . . this state of consciousness in which poetic emotion is created, as it were, at its source and from which it bursts forth without warning in great disorder . . .[32]

Thus we discover the key to a singular problem. From the moment that both Jaloux and Breton see in the image an inner revelation, coming before any language, and Souday and Prévost see a combination of words and sentences arising from an idea, we should no longer be surprised that one condemns images while the other praises them. It is their agreement that would be inexplicable, not their opposition. Each of them is merely applying the same secret view. But they use two different languages to express it, and two different frames of mind, between which no communication is possible. They are left with nothing but contempt, and do not shy from expressing it. (Yet it is an almost mechanical contempt, with an obvious cause, and not something to be proud of.)

We have seen both the cause and the remedy for this contempt. Of course, it is not possible for us to think overtly that form and content are one and the same thing, and that a word is an idea; but we may at least think "the hem of the skies" or "the dew with the head of a tabby cat" *as if* words were ideas, and form were content. We may think these things indirectly. We may, in fact, only think them indirectly. After all, because the contradiction is inevitable anyway (and all direct observation utterly fanciful), the key is in a way a compromise, almost a pact with this contradiction, which situates it in the only place where we can hope to understand it.

c) Poetry's own[33]

We had occasion to observe in passing how the most elementary language was, just like poetry, never without some mystery. We found an indirect proof of this (but we know that the event, for that matter, cannot be proved or grasped in any direct way) in the fact that linguists, because they fail to anticipate this mystery and find a place for it beforehand in their calculations, fall prey to it. They find themselves its dupes (being unable to be its scientists or engineers), as do the doctrinarians of poetry, who are all condemned to the same confusion. Moreover, this was nothing more than the discovery of something already well known, and poets have never stopped claiming that they were capable, as new Adams, of starting the primordial act of language afresh by imposing names on things. Yet we see that we have come to a new difficulty.

For if the same mystery really does happen in this, that, and the other place—in the cry, the conversation, the tale, in prose as in poetry—immediately we must ask ourselves why it is that, in poetry, it is more striking (perhaps more unexpected?) or in any case, according to common opinion, purer and seemingly more sensational. Why is it that the mystery is a natural part of this poetry's definition, and that we do not feel the same pride in conducting some precious spiritual experiment every time we speak and think?

Here, I would rather not risk a hypothesis. Instead, I will stick to simple description.

If, in order to explain this difference, I look for some obvious feature of poetry, I find this: it is that the poem offers, down to its last detail, a necessity that an ordinary sentence does not have. It makes more or less no difference whether we say: "You want 10 cents. Here they are." Or: "Here are the 10 cents you wanted." Or again: "You asked me for 10 cents. I am giving them to you." And we can imagine a thousand other analogous sentences. But change or move even a single word of

> *La fille de Minos et de Pasiphaë*[34]
> The daughter of Minos and Pasiphae

and something unique is lost forever—the very thing that guaranteed the charm and value of the verse, the very thing that *made* the verse. The line seems, rather than a sentence, like a word, whose letters could be neither changed nor modified without taking away its very nature. Yet it is not exactly a word, but a sum, a combination of various words, within which each maintains a certain degree of autonomy, and even puts up with being examined individually, as sometimes happens in the close reading of texts. The fact remains that this explanation is never entirely satisfying, or complete. It is as if the synthesis of these words were endowed with a new property that was not in the elements.

The same goes, in another domain, for volume in relation to space, for space in relation to line. For a volume is made of planes, and a plane of lines. And yet there is *also* in the volume something that was not in the planes, and in the planes something that was not in the lines: a new quality, which analysis immediately takes away.

I have talked only about raw language. There can be little doubt that the same observations would be true of thought, and that the line of verse, once created, requires that Minos remain precisely the son of Zeus and Europa, that Pasiphae remain Apollo's daughter and the bull's lover. In short, meaning, as soon as it is fixed, shows on the whole the same necessary character as words. We find, within meaning, the same movements and echoes back and forth, the complicity of distant elements, the intimate exchanges. Word and meaning, each in its own right, is torn away from its common condition and fixed in a new relation, one that is for the latter particularly thought out, and for the former essentially linguistic, and in which each achieves a higher intensity within the domain either of language or of thought.

What did we learn, however, from the mystery, if not that both words and meaning are therein *deprived* of their distinctive signs: of their nature. This mystery is the event (I mean this in the vaguest sense) and, precisely, the metamorphosis, thanks to which, words stop being accessible to our senses and lose their weight, their noise, their outline, their space (in order to become thought). But thought, for its part, relinquishes (in order to become words) its speed, be it fast or slow, its surprise, its invisibility, its time, and the inner consciousness we had of it. Such that the poem, or the verse, which endeavors on the contrary to provide the word, precisely, with a new sound and weight—with a more accomplished matter, but also, conversely, to provide meaning with a more pronounced and assured consciousness (thus strengthening both words and meaning according to their very nature)—cannot but seem to us an enterprise set against this mystery, and one that tends to restrict its play.

Here, a comparison can be of help. Let us imagine that a man runs a clearly defined risk: late-night attack, public contempt, or legal prosecution. He can simply run away. He can also protect himself from danger by joining forces with other men: clients, friends, accomplices in high places, all ready to protect him and supporting his cause, thus constituting another society whose center he occupies, with new bonds and relations, with its own rights and duties, devoted to his survival. Or else (depending on the nature of the risk) he will surround himself with obstacles and barricades, with an entire system of defense that the alleged enemy will be obliged to destroy before getting to him.

Metaphysicians sometimes imagine that the geometrical point, when threatened with dissolution—with returning to nothingness—creates a line from dots, a plane from the lines, a three-dimensional volume from the planes, at every step countering the risks of death or metamorphosis (as does a man in danger) with an additional obstacle or difficulty. Because the mysterious possibility of ruin, before it attacks the plane, will need to destroy the volume, destroy the plane before it attacks the line, and the line before the point. In the same way, the poet who cleverly assembles his commonplace expressions, antitheses, and apostrophes, or on the contrary sets free an unconscious mind he continually wants to make, and does, more foreign to him, ensures that the mystery, if it comes, will need henceforth to destroy his commonplaces before it destroys his words, his verses before his commonplaces—before his verses, the poem's very outline and design.

Here, however, lies the surprise and the paradox: despite every possible precaution, the crime is punished, the point dissolved, and the mystery and the metamorphosis happen. Thus it would seem that the passage of the mystery—so solid were the guarantees taken against it—would be all the more unexpected in poetry as the poem was a wiser and better-calculated precaution against it. It would be all the more striking as we had taken away its every chance of happening; all the more indisputable because the mechanism against it was stronger and better assembled—and we are all the more bedazzled before it. If Amphion's lyre only sends a speck of dust flying, one can say that it was the wind that did it. But if it sends a big chunk of stone flying . . . the poem, quite obviously, is rather more like the big chunk of stone.

In short, if we accept (as appears to be obvious) that the mystery is in some way necessary for our everyday language to play and breathe, the poem is like a gust of fresh air suddenly coming to us after we have nearly been suffocated through our own fault—like salvation when we are lost, like a joy deep in our crime. And surely it is not casually that we compare poetry to a purer air. But to someone who was on the verge of suffocation, any air seems pure. Such is the strange drama of poetry that the poet finds himself humiliated after so many efforts—and yet sides with the source of his humiliation. He is defeated, and delighted to be. He joins forces with what has defeated him, satisfied by what has outdone him. If he believes himself to be language's master, it is undoubtedly because even the humblest expression nearly failed him; he cannot imagine that language could ever court a greater danger than the one to which he has just exposed it—and from which he saves it.

I said that I had no intention of formulating some new theory in poetry. Here, at least, the event confirmed my words. I did not formulate a single new theory. I was simply led to propose, with the key, a new distribution of the same elements, whose presence in poetry is recognizable to all. It remains to apply this key to the various commentaries, secrets, themes, and doctrines that are currently heard about poetry.

Our purpose, here, is not to proceed with this application. It will be enough to have discovered on what condition a law of poetry has a chance of being true—on what condition as well (but it so happens that these conditions are one and the same) it can be understood exactly. Finally, it will be enough to have isolated, as an example, a first law—incidentally the most general law of all, because by definition it governs the various rules and constants that will be suggested later on.

Indeed, we could have discussed questions that were more pressing and of more immediate interest. We could have asked ourselves, for instance, what features distinguish poetry from poetic prose, a good poem from a bad one, and the fair critic from the unfair. But these are all questions to which we have given an answer as we went along—if at least one accepts (and who would not?) that the precise solution to a clearly defined problem is all the more valid for the vague and confused forms (the most basic ones) of the same problem. Thus we shall state that the work will be poetical, and the poem excellent, to the same extent that its words and ideas are—all things being equal (I mean to say: the mystery not being interrupted)—endowed, each in its own order, with the most complex structure. As for the reader or the critic, we have seen how I found myself (unless I am mistaken) being him, rather than defining him. But here is one final word.

Pascal emphasizes in the *Pensées* how philosophers, in general, readily confuse ideas and words, sometimes speaking of the body as if it were the mind, sometimes of the mind as if it were the body. No doubt, and not without reason. So do linguists, as we have seen; and poets and critics. They do this *so regularly* that this confusion had to appear to us as being our most constant reaction in matters of language: so constant that we were able to make of it, not an endpoint, as if our research were satisfied by it, as is usually the case, but rather its point of departure and its hidden part: managing to make the same dark corner in our thoughts about poetry correspond to its shadowy zone—allowing for what some physiologists call, in speaking of the eye, the same blind spot. This is the price we pay if poetry is to become clear to us, like all the things of this world to our eyes.

II

On Politics and Resistance

DEMOCRACY CALLS ON THE FIRST TO COME ALONG

This text was first published in the *Nouvelle Revue Française* (no. 306), March 1, 1939. The title poses several obstacles to translation in English, not least among them the semantic reach of the French phrase *le premier venu,* which is at once more nuanced and more common than any single English equivalent (see the translator's note). The original text is included in the *Œuvres complètes,* volume 5, pp. 277–81.

DEMOCRACY CALLS ON THE FIRST TO COME ALONG[1]

Translated by Jennifer Bajorek

Not least curious among the effects of triumphant fascisms is the anxiety into which they can plunge a democracy, dazzled by such success, vaguely jealous, quite willing to put water in the people's wine, and already convinced that its downfall has been an excess of democracy. But I am inclined to think it has been its lack.

DEMOCRACY'S SECRET

If I try to reduce democracy to its essential features, here is what I find:

The first thing is that the individual is greater than the state; and that society is made for man, and not man for society. The world is not wanting for sociologists to believe that every nation has a soul. Nor are unanimists, who argue that every group is a god, in short supply. Nor are Realpoliticians, who will tell you that the fasces alone is moral, just, potent. But democracy was invented despite sociologists, despite Realpoliticians, and even despite unanimism. Whatever the reason for our existence—the astonishing things that can happen to us, whatever gives us the right to life and, sometimes, to death—at least democracy knows *where* the reason is located, *where* the event comes to pass. In a word, it gives itself the person, and for it the person is enough. This is the first point.

It is a question of *any* person, be his skin black or red—this is the second point. Be he weak, drunk, treacherous. For democracy is as staunchly opposed to racism as it is to totalitarian regimes. It asserts that there is a strange quality to man, one that he will never be able entirely to reject (not even the convicted felon). The Declaration of Rights says that men are born equal—which it is easy enough to accept. It adds that they *stay* this way, which is a rather more singular thing to say. But this singularity, too, is part of the doctrine. Democracy has its mystery, like a religion, and it has its secret, like a poetry.

Here is the last thing about this secret: it is that a man counts for those parts of himself that are natural, immediate, naive, rather than for what he acquires. A great scholar has merit, but a man pure and simple is more precious than a great scholar, and even more extraordinary.

If you want to build a bridge, a castle, or a newspaper, you will gladly find yourself an architect, an engineer, or a journalist. But to build a nation, it is necessary to turn, first of all, to the man who is neither a journalist nor an architect. To the man in the street, who might just as well be a day laborer or a fruit vendor, or nothing at all. Democracy calls, despite the aristocrats—and especially despite the aristocrats of the intellect—on *the first to come along*. And it is not hard to see why: the first comer has stayed close to what matters most. A linguist can spend his whole life searching for the origin of language (he is mistaken). An architect can be obsessed, so much so that it haunts him in his dreams, by a concert hall in which concerts sound the way they should. But the man in the street has, for his part, only common joys and sorrows and accidents (and the accident, in particular, of which I spoke before). He must be happy with these things. He must be satisfied with them.

Democracy is like this also. I am not saying it is sensible or rational. I am not trying to convince anyone. Besides, it is perfectly obvious that we are not living in a democracy.

SEEING THAT EVERYONE IS HAPPY

The events of September have brought us a number of works and discourses, some of which are called *It's Your Own Business; Total Disgrace; Someday You'll Wake Up, Italians,* and others bearing no titles at all. But they might all be called, even more accurately, *The Disgrace of Munich As Seen through the Eyes of a Know-It-All,* or *Munich and Me,* or better: *None of this Would Have Happened If You'd Listened to Me.* They are every last one of them in agreement on this point. Mr. Marcel Thiébaut has painstakingly demonstrated, in *La Revue de Paris,* with the texts to support him, that there has not been one event in the last twenty years that could not have been predicted by the Count of Fels. But we knew it. We are all the Count of Fels. And Messrs. André Chaumeix, Henri Massis, Aragon, Mounier, Jean-Richard Bloch, and Jean Schlumberger have made the case, no less convincingly, that there has not been one catastrophe that France would not have avoided had it followed the advice of *La Revue des Deux Mondes,* of *La Revue universelle,* of *Commune,* of *Europe,* of *Esprit,* and even the (to be sure much more modest) advice of the *NRF.* If I am citing the reviews, it is because they have the time for reflection, and for second thoughts. But it goes without saying that the newspapers have been even more satisfied with themselves.

I am not inclined to irony, and if I were, I would save the irony for a more fitting occasion. For the fact is *they are all telling the truth.* This is astounding, and I think we ought to be more worried about it. In short, everything is happening as if France *had never followed anyone's advice.* For there is not *a single* policy that—had it been firmly enforced from 1920 forward—could not have spared us the disgrace of this recent Munich, and of every Munich to come.

Charles Maurras, Bainville, and Massis had hoped, as early as 1917, to preserve a strong Austro-Hungarian empire but a partitioned Germany under the supervision of a government of our choosing. This would have been an intelligent and sensible policy. At the same time, Herriot, Paul-Boncour, and Jean Schlumberger held, as early as 1920, that what we should do was hand all moral and material authority over to the League of Nations; that we should remove certain injustices from the peace treaty of our own accord; that, having disarmed Germany, we should disarm ourselves, and prove at long last that the Allies were not lying when they declared peace in the world. This policy would have been intelligent and just. And the same holds for all the rest. For Jules Romains, Flandin, and Bergery argued, in 1934, that we should take Chancellor Hitler at his word, by openly accepting a partial disarmament when he was still respecting treaties. Why not? (This would have been our reconciliation with Germany, perhaps one that would have lasted.) Léon Blum, Aragon, and Jean-Richard Bloch maintained, in 1935, that we should choke off, in ten days, by means of merciless sanctions, the people who had just violated the freely accepted law. That may well have been true. (And the whole world would no doubt have gone along.) Finally, Maurice Thorez, Emmanuel Mounier, and Julien Benda hoped, in 1936, that a sudden French intervention in Spain would save a friendly government from fascist rebellion. Granted. (This would most likely have been the best protection for our border.) In addition to which, neither the Italian alliance nor the embassy at Burgos were in themselves foolish projects. Still, they would have had to be implemented.

All these good intentions and not even a hell emerges. Scarcely even a morass. For it is patently obvious that we should have decided on one of these courses—even the most mediocre—and stuck fiercely to it. But we chose instead to do them all, half-heartedly, at once: to humiliate Germany and to let it multiply its strength tenfold. To grant Italy God knows what hypocritical favors and to injure it publicly. To feign support for the League while making it a laughingstock. To give Spain covert aid—not enough to save it, but enough to compromise ourselves. To grant a powerful Germany what we had refused a defenseless one. As if there were, in these promises made to everyone, in this spurious reconciliation of differences, a consistent political tactic.

If I speak of foreign policy, it is because the question is in the air. I might just as well be talking about the muck in the streets and the birthrate. Our deputies and our ministers are honest people—and more than one city is administered by bandits. Good urbanists—and Paris is surrounded by a slum. Tasteful—and the interior of the French home is hideously ugly. Enthusiastic—and France does not celebrate holidays.

There is no point in asking, with any seriousness, what this kind of conduct will bring, or whether it is wise. It is idiotic. But we might ask ourselves whether it is democratic.

Well, it is not. It is even quite the opposite.

THE PRINCE OF INTELLECT AND THE MAN IN THE STREET

It has occasionally been argued that it is necessary, in matters of politics, to take every personal opinion into account. But this was in the Diet of Poland, which was composed of nobles, as everyone knows. From time immemorial, there have been philosophers to show that there is truth to every doctrine. But the man in the street has always thought that there is, in all things, one true opinion, and that the contrary opinion is false. The intellectual is a person who gets along just fine without holidays, and who thinks that slums have poetic charm. But the ordinary man slices his Twelfth Night cake and likes his room to be clean. The sophisticate is able to delight in humiliation, and to feel he is the better for it. But the man in the street is miffed: he resolves (as he puts it) to nurse his grudge. The law professor soberly demonstrates in *Le Temps* that there is a tacit subtext in every treaty, and that we should betray, in 1938, the agreements we made in 1935 because the world situation has changed. But the ordinary man quite simply accepts that, in abandoning a friend he has endangered, he acts like a snake.

In short, no sooner are you faced with a baroque and manifestly ridiculous opinion than you can be sure it was the brainchild of some prince of thought. Professors of the Collège de France have established that wars were caused by gun dealers (and doubtless, in olden days, by dealers in bows or in boiling oil). A great English thinker has maintained indefatigably, for thirty years, that wars have never benefited anyone, the victor least of all. (Mr. Aldous Huxley has just now rallied to this theory, which Mr. Jules Romains has ceaselessly extolled.) The most distinguished economists, the toast of all Europe, proved, around 1910, that under no circumstances could the hostilities continue for more than two months, because there was not enough money. And Mr. Léon Blum has always argued that all we need do is get rid of armies to put an end to war. This is what the men of genius have to say. But the bricklayer, the bus driver, and the doorman on the corner have always known that a war can be waged very well without money (and that the economists will sort it out afterward) and that armies, or even boiling oil or guns, are not the primary cause of wars. Well, in a proper democracy, it is to the bricklayer that the decision must fall. But no, we have princes deciding everything for us.

We know by what methods. All this patient labor that is going on, in France, in the committees and the lodges, in the cells and the working groups, in the sections and the subsections of our great parties, this labor that gives rise to the nominations and the candidates, the deputies and the senators, the votes of the deputies and the senators, the laws, and even our foreign policy—we can praise it no end. It is intelligent and persistent, studious and (for the most part) disinterested, subtle and all-embracing. It mobilizes millions of texts and documents. It calls on hundreds of thousands of men. In the end, you can say any and everything you like about it, except one thing. It is not democratic. It breeds and painstakingly cultivates an aristocracy of knowledge, of intellect, and of eloquence. And God forbid that I speak ill of intelligence. We need it. We need scholars and specialists. It is just that I think—if, at any rate, I am a democrat—that in those situations where the specialists and the scholars disagree (as they are in the habit of doing) the last word should go—rather than to a mongrelized agreement among specialists that apparently makes everyone happy and does no one any good—to the Arbitration, to the Despotism of someone who is neither learned, nor artful, nor a genius, nor especially gifted with eloquence, nor a star pupil, nor the champion of any sport. Of someone who does not owe his station to his dazzling merits, or to his charm, or to a plebiscite. Of, I will say it again, the first to come along.

As for designating this first person, this is an altogether different matter. We might imagine, to fix the idea in some form, one of those abstract deputies of whom Vigny spoke—deputies, not of Niort or of Romorantin, but simply of France. Eight or ten would be enough. One would be enough.

THE BEE

This text first appeared in *Les Cahiers de la Libération* during the German occupation of France, on February 29, 1944, and was signed, as were many of the texts published therein, with a pseudonym—in this case "Juste," or "the Just." The original text appears in the *Œuvres complètes,* volume 5, pp. 287–88.

THE BEE

Translated by Jennifer Bajorek

Had we been occupied (to use the polite term) by the Swedish, at least we'd be left with a dance step, a taste for yellow and blue ribbons; by the Javanese, with a way of wiggling the fingers; by the Hottentots, the Italians, the Hungarians, we'd be left with a song, a smile, a little nod of the head. In a word, with one of these silly mannerisms that mean nothing in particular—that signify simply that one is happy to be alive, that one prefers this to not living at all, and that it is fun (above all) to have a body, from which we are able to draw so much whimsical pleasure.

But they, it is plain to see, will leave us nothing. Not a song, not a funny face. Even the kid in the street doesn't propose to imitate the goose step (which has become, along with waiting in line at the grocery, our way of living together). They never bump into anyone, as we are likely, alas, to continue to do. They even pick up the packages that careless people drop. And yet, they don't make us want to pick any packages up. They are soulless. They will have passed like a big void. As if they were already dead. Except that they spread this death all around them. It is even the one thing they do with skill.

That they seem to us so utterly transparent is sometimes said to be a result of our dignity. I'd like to think so. I've read in books (the best editions) that an honest Frenchwoman can lodge the noblest occupier in her house for six months (and even fall mildly in love with him) without even once saying "hello." But surely this is an exceptional Frenchwoman. I myself don't feel so dignified (nor so quick to fall in love). And then, the French in general haven't been so dignified.

One must not forget that France is, in principle, not at war. It is a kind of neutral country, whose capital is Vichy. And we have no qualms—fortunately!—when it comes to telling the truth about the people of Vichy, which is that they are bastards. But we feel a certain solidarity with them all the same. There is, in each of us, a part that—grudgingly—

understands them; that doesn't take them to be out and out fools; that sometimes goes so far as to wonder whether Vichy wasn't a ploy to save Algeria, and whether Pétain wasn't monstrously shrewd (and then immediately reproaches itself for having thought it); that finds itself compelled, moreover, to make allowances for them. Because those of us who are fighting are not under any obligation but are acting with the perfect merit and pure nobility of the soldier (which the official wars had very nearly obscured).

So those of us, at least, who are not fighting might consent to have a good time (if they could show us one). To learn something (if they were teaching us anything). But we see that on this count too (it is nothing to be proud of) we are disappointed. That everything is happening as if they were already dead. But—I'm back to this—it is a death that they spread.

When I was a child, I was (like all children) surprised to find announced in the back pages of the newspaper many more deaths than births. (The explanation—although we don't consider this until later—is of course that it is rare, except in the case of kings, for someone to be very well known at birth, whereas for the famous man, it remains only to die.) I also had the sense that all of this had just changed. The trend was rather more toward births. People were dying much less.

The notion is absurd. I nonetheless think that I have, in some vague way, hung on to it, that it is quite common, that it plays a part in the sorrow of a time in which we learn, every month, of the death of some friend. One joined the maquis; they found his body in a field, already bloated. Another was printing pamphlets, yet another was carrying notes: they shot them full of bullets when they talked. Others endured, before they died, tortures surpassing in horror what a person with cancer or with tetanus suffers.

And I know that there are those who say: they died for almost nothing.[1] A simple point of information (not always very accurate) wasn't worth that, or a pamphlet, not even an underground paper (often rather poorly put together). To such people, I can only respond: "It's that they were on the side of life. It's that they loved things as insignificant as a song, a snap of the fingers, a smile. You can squeeze a bee in your hand until it suffocates to death. But it won't die without stinging you first. That hardly matters, you say. Yes, it hardly matters. But if it didn't sting you, the bees would be long gone."

LETTER ON PEACE

The text was published in *Liberté de l'Esprit* (no. 6), in the summer of 1949. *Liberté de l'Esprit* was a periodical belonging to a new press affiliated with the Rassemblement du Peuple Français (RPF). The RPF was founded in 1947 by Gen. Charles de Gaulle who, after resigning his leadership of the *gouvernement provisoire* in 1946, was increasingly involved in a struggle over what he considered to be the necessary transformation of the Fourth Republic's institutions. The RPF was, significantly, opposed to the French Communist Party. The text is included in the *Œuvres complètes,* volume 5, pp. 407–12.

LETTER ON PEACE

Translated by Charlotte Mandell

Dear Sir,

I have thought more than once about your investigation: it has provided the opportunity for me to do some soul-searching. Who am I, after all, to deserve to reply to you? A simple grammarian, who scarcely gets on any better in politics than in ethics. It is true that I desire peace, as does everyone else. But I desire it timidly, and, if I can say so, secretly. When I hear the brave M. Philip state that this peace is a question of life or death for us, or the excellent M. Spaak during a fine declamation: "We want peace, and we will not let ourselves be attacked by anyone!" or else the delightful Paul Eluard: "We are fighting against war," I am embarrassed. They are right, of course. Yet it seems to me that peace is driven off by battles, by questions of life and death, by fine declamations, who knows, perhaps even by speeches. . . .

I'll come back to that. In fact, I am of a rather peculiar breed of grammarians.

1.
ON A GRAMMAR OF IDEAS

Why the devil did we invent grammar books? It isn't simply, as we usually think, to bother schoolchildren. Or at least to keep them busy. No. It is because it has happened to each of us: we've had the very definite feeling that a sentence is well or poorly constructed; a word, used rightly or wrongly. It is a very decisive feeling, one we ordinarily wouldn't fail to express right away, in a more or less heated way (and children aren't the least heated about this).

We have to live with these feelings. We have to get used to them. So grammarians decide to observe them. They acknowledge them, insofar as possible, and in the end insert in their books all they have gathered from the conversation of good, or bad, society. This is what I want to address.

Namely this: just as we are affected by words, we are affected by the thoughts presented to us every day. A cousin overwhelms us with good advice, a friend exposes us to his political opinions, a girlfriend demonstrates to us that we were very wrong to suspect her. We listen. And after five minutes we experience a curious impression: that the statements given us are correct, linked together, coherent—and yet completely idiotic. Logical, but absurd. So absurd as to be obvious: no less obvious than a grammatical mistake.

Yes, well, we can also have quite the opposite impression: when someone presents us with illogical, even incoherent, statements, but ones that nonetheless are found to be—we don't really know why—entirely fair, perfectly true. No, we don't know why. But after all, we could very easily find out. It shouldn't be so difficult. It is, in a word, feelings of this nature that I would like to pin down. It seems to me that it should be possible to collect them, to acknowledge them, to make, from their collection—just as there exists a grammar of words and phrases—a grammar of ideas. And I can't say I've gotten very far in my task. I work, I do what I can. That's all one can reasonably ask of me.

As to the rest, note that I don't have any illusions. The method used is an austere one, not at all cheerful. Not encouraging. I hope it will lead me to some certainties. But they will be—from all appearances—somewhat meager certainties: in any case, deprived of those generous enthusiasms and flights of eloquence that are awakened in us by the big questions: peace, freedom, Europe, etc. Deprived, in any case, of the flabbiness and confusion that usually follow: of that horrible dumping ground of touching thoughts and good feelings, that stir nothing in us but a violent wish to riposte with insults and jokes.

We'll leave that for now. The fact remains that the method requires a certain detachment. Even a certain cynicism. One has to take sides once and for all. There are, I know, problems and dangers that are so moving that simply by keeping a cool head one seems guilty of indifference. And I am not saying that is an unfair feeling in any respect. But one must first of all keep a cool head, even if it's only to discover that the feeling is not entirely unfair. The hotter the danger, the cooler one must keep one's head. But I'm coming to your question.

2. IN WHICH THE BEST ARGUMENTS ARE OVERTURNED

I think we should rank bad reasoning—generated every day by the anxiety to put an end to wars—at the top of the list of horrors of wars.

First a famous economist demonstrates to us, with statistics to back him up, that we have to renounce war because it "doesn't pay," but bankrupts both combatants. But even if I set aside the very baseness of the argument, I see the opposite is true. Never have Russia or the United States been so powerful as they are today, or so prosperous. That might not count for much. (It is indeed a question of statistics!) Never, though, have the Russians or the Americans had a better conscience. And who would dare to argue that Hitler, if he had won the victory and world empire—he missed it by a hair's breadth—would not have won anything!

Then they direct our attention to the prodigious number of people who were massacred; to the irreparable voids that are thus hollowed out within the nations' populations. The unfortunate thing is that the argument is worthless. There is no void that isn't soon filled: the appalling losses of Russia in 1914 were compensated for, and more, by 1917. France numbers more inhabitants today than it did in 1939. War in the history of a people has the same gravity as a bout of measles in a family with fifteen children.

And then they recount every kind of misery that war engenders. They mention the crippled and the mutilated, their eyes gouged out, their bellies torn open. They add that more bombs will multiply torture and ruin ad infinitum. Indeed. But have you reflected that men are courageous? (And perhaps foolhardy. Or at least adventurous.) Add to that, though, the fact that they want to prove their courage every day—to others and to themselves. The more horrible your descriptions, the more you offer them the chance they've been dreaming of.

But that still would be nothing, if they didn't have the best reasons—and, in their eyes, the noblest—to display this courage. Imagine that they are going to seize this opportunity and give it their all; that there are not many men who aren't ready to fight for vengeance if they have been conquered, for justice if they are oppressed, for their independence if they are slaves, for their dignity, if they think they have been offended. You want the surest proof of this? Ask today's pacifists: "So should we have yielded to Hitler?" They reply in the negative. But you could find

Hitler again tomorrow. Poor arguments, that don't hold up before the next fact that comes along.

I will imagine, though, that you have convinced me. I in turn state that I am against war. And against warmongers. What does that mean, and what can I do to fight a warmonger? Give him good advice? He lets me go on. Exile him from humanity? He couldn't care less. Threaten him with civil war? "Don't bother yourself about it," he says. "That's my business, I'll put everything in order." Have him sentenced by a supreme court? He is unmoved. What's left? To declare war on him.

Note that at this point all your arguments are overturned. War is atrocious? I have to make it even more atrocious, to make my enemy disgusted with it forever. War doesn't pay? I will make it pay, this time, by my terrible demands. War depopulates the world? At least let it depopulate the world of the bellicose! Strange, these arguments for peace, which become valid only in the service of war.

3. WHOEVER WANTS PEACE, PREPARES FOR WAR

As I have said, the grammar of ideas has yet to be written, and I offer these remarks as they come to me: off the top of my head. They barely have the merit of being obvious. Here, though, is something that could give them weight: that the authors—there's no shortage of them—of "Treatises on Perpetual Peace" clearly stumble on the difficulty. If you desire peace, begin by waging war: Henri IV (and later on the good Father Gratry) want to bring peace to Europe. Listening to them, it would be enough for Christians to get along together: first, chase out the Turks, exterminate them if necessary. However, Leibniz or the Abbé de Saint-Pierre dream instead of a Holy Alliance among monarchs. And if some sovereign refused to join? Or some people refused to follow its sovereign? They will soon be made to see reason. (Funny, this language, in which war is called *reason*.) Later on, Kant, Anatole France, or Romain Rolland will go as far as peace for the entire world: all that has to be done, they say, is once and for all to win the nations over to a political system in which each subject is a citizen: to impose it on them if necessary. But this won't happen without battles. Don't be too surprised at that. We are living in a world where the word *Peace!*—if it said with even a grain of authority—means pretty much: "I'm going to smack you."

But do we have to go and consult writers? It's enough for me to observe the parties, and the various governments. Scarcely had the Reformation proposed to go back to the peace of Primitive Christianity when it began to soak Germany and Europe with blood. The French Revolution had only to declare peace to the entire world before it saw itself forced to wage twenty years of war. Not only this, but they created for that war the most pitiless army system ever conceived: compulsory military service. The czar had no sooner established his Court of Peace than he began to fight. And we all know how the League of Nations ended up: the least you can say is that it came to a bad end. Every era has excellent minds that try to research where wars come from. The answer is simple: they come from the dogged passion for making peace treaties that every now and then overcomes men.

I do not mean particular, modest kinds of peace, peace that is more or less well-constructed. No: I mean general peace. We have to admit that we've made appreciable progress on that account, in a few years. Hypocrisy gives way a little more every day, and the big peace conferences with their doves, the announcements for which we've seen plastered on our walls, don't much try anymore to pass themselves off for what they're not. The motto of Mr. Joliot-Curie, of Paul Eluard, and of the Communists might just as well be: "Any war, except against Russia." (I don't know what joker proposed, in the Pleyel auditorium, that we put an end to the war in China. It was badly received.) However, the motto of Mr. Churchill, of Mr. Spaak, and of the major Europeans might on the contrary be: "Any war, except against America." I say nothing of Messieurs Sartre and Rousset, with their *Rassemblement démocratique*.[1] They are simply proposing to replace national wars with civil wars. Don't have any illusions: the birth of this, if we are to believe M. Rousset, will be "bloody."

All these people who talk about peace are thinking only about our blood.

I said just now, and it is all too obvious, that peace finds questions of life and death, battles, fine declamations, political speeches repellent. More: it is quite possible that it is repulsed by desire itself, and clear reflection.

Whoever strongly desires peace is already clenching his fists. Whoever steadily craves it creates a war machine.

We are living through singular times, where each individual firmly believes there is no illness of society or of the mind that resists knowledge, or the illumination of its motivating forces—that resists the full light of day. Everyone believes this, and no one can say that the results of this are very happy. But what if the opposite were true? What if there existed evils that come from too much light, and thoughts that have to be made a little dimmer to give themselves fully? If there were really only one hope for peace: that it be silent rather than expressed, and somehow prayed for rather than demonstrated. It would already be an important result of the grammar of which I spoke to you, if it led us to this discovery.

LETTER TO THE DIRECTORS ABOUT EUROPE

The text was published in December 1949, also in *Liberté de l'Esprit* (no. 7) and is included in the *Œuvres complètes,* volume 5, pp. 413–25.

LETTER TO THE DIRECTORS ABOUT EUROPE

Translated by Charlotte Mandell

I happened one day to take a plane for Nice at Le Bourget. At the appointed time, the machine began to shake, then made for a road that was clearly marked between two fields. It was raining. The plane slowed down, turned around, and bravely started up again on the road it had already traveled. We progressed at the average speed of an automobile. The plane turned to the left, then to the right. (This airfield has as many roads as a freight yard has train tracks.) But then the rain stopped. Suddenly we saw the sun. We also saw that the machine was rolling along noisily over a cluster of clouds, and we all understood that in the meantime we had taken off.

A few seconds later, a surprising thing happened. A little eight-year-old girl asked, loud enough to be heard over the noise of the engine: "Mom, are we going to start flying soon?" That's exactly what I had been thinking. The mother answered with some silly remark. Thus it is with Europe.

1.
THERE IS EUROPE AND THERE IS EUROPE

For two hundred years now philosophers, orators, poets—and even a few dry economists—have been vociferously announcing to us the United States of Europe. Well, it seems they've gotten there. We don't have to look any further. The Council of Europe met in Strasbourg a few weeks ago. It already has its statute (consisting of forty-two articles); its Committee of Ministers (for the executive); its consulting Assembly (for deliberations); its Secretariat (for the preparatory work). In short, it lacks nothing. Absolutely nothing, except bearing any resemblance to Europe.

For it does not resemble Europe in the least. To tell the truth, it is hard to see why the people of Strasbourg had the idea of calling "Europe" an association of countries that does not include Russia, or Poland, or Czechoslovakia, or Rumania, or Hungary, or Spain, or Finland, or Greece, or (until now) Germany and Yugoslavia. Or even Switzerland! (Which, nonetheless, is our model.) But which contains the English Empire (with England), the French Empire (with France), Turkey, Ireland, and seemingly—although it scarcely makes an appearance—the United States of America. One would say it was a joke. A little eight-year-old girl can see right away that it doesn't resemble Europe any more than a locomotive resembles a bird: it comprises at best a quarter, scarcely a thin sliver, from the North Cape to the Adriatic. But she has been told often enough that Europe, the real Europe, ended in the Urals. We are not going to go and tell her the opposite now.

That's enough physical geography. But from the moral point of view (if I may say), the resemblance is even more tenuous.

For finally one can be led to form a union for many different reasons: because there is mutual affection (with all the attendant pledges); because we're going to get something out of it; or simply because the various parties were compromised in the same unfortunate affair: for instance, if they were arrested on the same day by the vice squad. It is this last way that we have chosen: a kind of reconciliation in crapulence. We Europeans have all gone bankrupt, even fraudulently.

War has ruined us, it is true. There were two very simple (and very moral) remedies for that: one was to tighten our belts and slave away like men possessed. (That is pretty much what Russia decided to do.) The other was to send a number of Europeans to go work in America, while America sent its assets to work here. We found a third way.

That was to make new debts every day, and to aggravate the bankruptcy. But at the same time to tear out our hair and shout on the rooftops that we were lost if the United States—the real one, not the European version—refused to come to our aid. That was accompanied by a gentle blackmail: "If you don't accept, we are all quite capable of throwing ourselves into the arms of Russia."

So the United States kindly gave in, yielding either to pity, or to blackmail (not counting the satisfaction of keeping clients in good shape). The fact is that they replied to us: "That's all right, you'll have your money. But first stop squabbling among yourselves! What do you think you look like?" That is how we saw ourselves forced to make Europe. Surely there were more dignified ways. And more prudent.

For finally what we have been led to hope for from Europe, for two hundred years, was, roughly, peace. Or at least a large step toward peace. But this Europe looks more to me like a war machine. What are you doing about Russia? Do you think it's possible to exclude it without doing it violence? Without at least giving it the feeling—as with Germany in '14—that you have it surrounded? Without thus inviting it to take up arms?

Or maybe you think you'll seduce it with your accords and your treaties. But these accords, under penalty of being void, will imply that the European government has a say in the armies and industries—who knows, even the press and the literature—of each nation. (Just to ensure that another war isn't being fomented in some corner.) Are you going to go ask Russia to show you its arsenals? Even its public squares are closed to you. To declare its military budget to you? It hides even its holidays and its laws from you.

I am telling you what everyone knows. Perhaps you will reply that there has never been a general peace that wasn't preceded by a major war. (But what if, for a time, we renounced general peace?) You will reply that it's a question of ensuring for France a choice place, in the forefront of the coming rout—and in the treaties that will follow. (But what if we renounced, at the same time, all routs?) Since the Germans fight so well, it's a question of inducing them to fight, for once, on the right side. . . .

Let's leave that aside. It still remains the case that you have botched your Europe. And why? What was there in your project that was false or idiotic—in all the projects for Europe that philosophers, orators, and poets, but especially, these days, the Federalists, have been forming for two hundred years?

We'll have to ask them.

2.
EUROPE AGAINST HOMELANDS

Well, in the main, they are pretty encouraging. So encouraging, even, that it starts to get a little suspicious. As if we really had to expect only celebrations and festivals.

And what festivals! Jean Guéhenno, he sees in a unified Europe the only means of ensuring with scant delay social justice (like the Russians) while still maintaining liberty (like the Americans). André Philip goes even further: the creation of a vast European market, by grouping 260 million buyers, will lower the cost price of commodities and raise the workers' quality of life. No more poverty! No more unemployment!

Denis de Rougemont, however, announces the end of despair and isolation, the death of national resentments. The Federation (he adds) will create a Europe of the West, fair enough to form, between Capitalist deception and Communist equivocation, a new social order—powerful enough to impose its neutrality on the whole world. There are subtler benefits from which these derive.

Jaspers in effect holds that European harmony alone will allow each of us to reflect—and hence organize—in complete freedom of mind: to remain masters of our thoughts, without subjugating them to any dogmatism. Jean de Salis: to reflect and express oneself according to one's own genius, with perfect dignity. Rougemont: to give oneself over without reservation to one's inner tensions, to become, a saint, a mystic, or a martyr, as one likes. (A fascist? No, I don't think that's an option.) In short, each of us will forget the national prejudices that clouded his mind a little, and will be all the freer to stir up the big problems.

That may be. But finally what price must we pay for so much good? Let us understand each other. Unification is in itself neither good nor bad. It all depends on who is unified, and with whom. We all know couples who would be better off if they weren't couples; and friends who, if they were honest, would break up this very day. It is not desirable (for the smooth running of societies) that murderers and common-law criminals—and who knows, maybe even bankrupts—should form associations with each other that are too close; nor should the big manufacturers. The union of Franche-Comté with France seems to have been a good union. But the union of Ireland with England was surely an execrable one, and has been abandoned. In fact, it seems that in Europe, in the past 150 years or so—since we've been beaten over the head a little with the United States of Europe—there have been more execrable unions than good ones: Norway got divorced from Sweden (not without bitterness); Belgium from Holland; Bohemia from Austria; Greece, Bulgaria, and Serbia from the Ottoman Empire. And so on. We have seen a number of countries born, whose names were completely unpronounceable. The doctrinarians, the Philips and Spaaks of that time,[1] were not embarrassed by such trifles; they invoked some principle or other. It had an important name, this name of "principle." If the Europe of this scheme showed some consistency and some will in the end, it was precisely a will for division and local patriotism.—But that is precisely it, the Federalists reply, it is this love of one's homeland we are attacking: love for those national idols to which Europe (according to Raymond Aron) "has just brought so much generosity, blood, and love as an offering."

Well, why don't you say it more bluntly?

There was a Federalist to say it, with all desirable bluntness. This was Julien Benda.

Benda begins by stating that Europe, if it is formed, will be the creation of intelligence, not of instinct. For instinct is particularist, and thus patriotic: it pushes each Frenchman (for instance) to become more deeply French—more stupidly French; to take pride only in a French history; to defend, for a French science, a reasoning that is more French every day; to want for France more glory and importance, more space in the sun (and for it to be talked about in all the newspapers).

That is where love of one's country leads. It is in each one of us, powerful and fertile with trickery. How is it to be conquered? Seemingly a kind of intelligence is required, which is not adaptable to our instincts, but decisive and firm; turned entirely toward morality (which is the province of no country); intimately convinced that the mind suffers from having a body, and the soul from having a nation. In short, an intelligence that is enamored of order and general truth.

"Press on" (says Benda to the Europeans). "Mistrust the natural enemies of this truth. I am not thinking just of soldiers, but of poets and artists—smitten by emotion, sensitive to the particular, attached to the unique (and hence in love with their nation and whatever original qualities it has). Heroism and agitation, love of mountains and of storms, that is what you have to vomit up first of all, if you want Europe—I won't say to be given a body, a body would always be too much, but at least to receive a soul."

There are two or three remarks to make about this. . . .

One is that Benda restricts himself, in short, to crudely setting forth in daylight the hidden arguments of the Federalists. The other is that these arguments all had good reasons to remain hidden. We'll pass up the mountains (what will the Swiss say?). But do we really have to renounce the surprises of heroism, the taste for invention, reading the poets? That's not much fun!

The last remark is more serious. It is that Benda is thoroughly mistaken. And along with him, I'm afraid, are the bulk of the Federalists. I don't mean, far from it, that Benda is an idiot: he has a clear, methodical intelligence, and he doesn't lack wit. But there does exist a whole range of feelings (coarse, or mysterious) about which you'd have to learn from someone who is clumsy, even a little doltish (like me). Or even from that grammar of perfectly common ideas, which I spoke of before.[2]

Morever, the question is vast: it goes well beyond Benda, and even patriotism.

3.
THEY HAVE NEVER BEEN IN LOVE

It is very true that we are every one of us born citizens (or subjects) of a very definite country: French, English, even Chinese or Laplanders.

And it is no less true that this accident of our birth could easily make us unfair—because of instinct, of which Benda speaks—toward someone who was a victim of a different accident. In fact, patriotism risks making us stupid. Good old Flaubert naively said: "The homeland has always seemed to me a boundless kind of stupidity. It consists in living on a patch of land marked in blue on the map, and in looking askance at the green or red patches."

This is true. It seems unarguable. To take things a step further: if I was born a man, well, I have to give up ever being a woman—and this closes off a good half of humanity to me. Nor can I be a gazelle, a bull, a poplar tree—and this closes off three quarters of life to me. Nor a river or a rock—nine-tenths of the world. But there's even worse, and your free choice (as you call it) is no less ill fated than chance. If you marry a woman, you give up (for the moment at least) all other women. You neglect a vertiginous number of women. If you happen imprudently to become a cabinetmaker or a journalist, you treat a thousand other respectable livelihoods unjustly: you refuse to be a sailor, a diplomat, or a professional dancer. You give up the great ocean spaces and the delights of intrigue. At every instant so many avenues and joys are necessarily closed to you. You can't go buy a pack of cigarettes at the bistro, at least not in my neighborhood (Jardin des Plantes), without scorning the giant frog (which is waiting for you in the Vivarium, just opposite), mint tea (which you could go drink at the mosque), the Seine (which it is so pleasant to watch flow by). It's enough to make you dizzy; suddenly you want nothing more than to stay there without budging. But that would be to refuse everything at once, to be unfair to everything: to the Seine and the frog, the mosque and even the packet of tobacco. That is indeed what makes life the most sinister adventure imaginable (if, that is, every pleasant event is accompanied by a hundred painful refusals—so that the scale always tips to the wrong side). Unless . . .

I have no opinion about such serious matters. But in the end what I see clearly is that we still and all haven't given up hope. Our natural grammar—our reflection in the face of reasoning and arguments—doesn't work. On the contrary, it maintains steadfastly that being a man is undoubtedly the best way to be able to put yourself (as close as we can get) in the place of a rock or a gazelle (and, of course, of a woman); and that in order to imagine the adventures of a sailor or a diplomat with emotion, it is not bad to stay peacefully at home (for neither the diplomat nor the sailor has the necessary distance: they cannot see themselves).

And so on. For the grammar of ideas also holds that Don Juan is ordinarily an intelligent character, inquisitive to a fault; but he has one defect that outweighs so many qualities: he doesn't know women very well; just as the world traveler doesn't know the individual countries. On the contrary, the grammar believes that for the man who is content with one single woman, every day she is like a new woman; and the good peasant who doesn't leave his field knows better than the world traveler what makes man human: fine weather and rain, friendship, family. (While the other lingers over vague stories about journeys on camelback, and accounts of anthropophagy.) I readily admit that here it is a matter of a paradoxical opinion. The whole problem lies in finding out if the paradox is true: if, in the heart of human nature, such a *recourse* truly exists—if man is really saved by the very thing that should ensure his loss, and if the homeland is not finally the best (or only) way to think about the world.

"Leave these heights," say (ironically) the Federalists. "You are not going to deny at least that an ill-considered love of country is at the origin of national hatreds and wars. Freud and Einstein have said so. Our professors and our economists, our sociologists and our politicians, repeat it every day. Read, rather, the investigations of the League of Nations, and those of the UN. You'll find nothing but nationalism. . . ." Precisely. I'm coming to that.

I am sorry to say it. But the truth is that the economists and sociologists in question, and even Freud and Einstein, don't know what love is.

They have never, from all appearances, been in love. I am not reproaching them. They have had a lot of other things to do, and life is so complicated these days! It's not easy to reach a high position, and that alone is enough to explain it. Moreover, they have surely been loved (even if only because of their great intelligence, or their good position)—I mean that they have let themselves be loved, but that's very different. If they had been in love, they would know what every little girl and boy in the street knows: namely that love—even if reciprocated—is rather a humble and terrified feeling. It doesn't make you at all proud or provocative. One doesn't speak to one's grocer with greater authority. One doesn't insist on being first in line. One doesn't feel ready to beat up one's neighbor. Quite the contrary: one would willingly do without neighbors and even without one's grocer. One would be content, as the proverb says quite correctly, with a little cottage and a heart. Now, the cottage is the smallest house one can have on earth, and a heart is smaller still. And I know that lovers readily call each other king and queen—this is probably what confuses the social theorists. It's a matter of an intimate sovereignty, that one doesn't want to impose on anyone. One doesn't even much try to make it public. It's enough to love, in order to have the somewhat confused (but very keen) sensation that the whole world is jealous of us.

Thus it is with homelands. The real lover of France would be content if all of France could be contained in Paris (or in Marseille, or in Douai. Douai, though . . .). To have to oneself a country so vast and so complicated that it spills over into Africa and Asia, obviously he gets used to it (since he has no choice), but it bothers him. He would willingly give it up, if he weren't afraid of upsetting it. Lovers are always saying to each other, "my little one," and the lover of France would like France to be little enough for him to hold it in his hand.

And I don't think the big conquerors will be offered to me as arguments. Hitler, Napoleon, Stalin may have been excellent or mediocre doctrinarians. They all had their recipes for peace in Europe and the world. They applied them with force. Not one man in his right senses would think to call them great nationalists. Unless he were mistaken, like a Federalist. But I'm telling you, that's life. You eat an apple (say the old myths) and paradise is lost. You make a slight mistake about love, and you get a Europe that resembles Europe as much as an automobile resembles a skylark. . . .

Yes, the mother replied that we had been flying for a quarter of an hour. She seemed sincere. She seemed above all not to have understood a single word of her daughter's question. *Flying,* everyone knows what that means: those rustlings and that ascension, the body (finally) become feathers ("How are you holding up?" "I can't hold myself up anymore"), those spaces free of vertigo, your spirit is delighted, as soon as you think about it. That really took some nerve to talk about flight, in referring to our aerial locomotive.

Still, since then we have discovered hang-gliding, and there is no reason not to think that Europe itself, if we came to having more precise ideas about the homeland . . .

LETTER TO THE DIRECTORS OF THE RESISTANCE

Paulhan was a member of the French Resistance to German occupation and cofounded, together with other prominent intellectuals, the clandestine National Committee of Writers (le Comité National des Écrivains, also known as the CNE, or Céné) in connection with his political activities of this period. This association had, by the time of the Liberation, gathered a great deal of moral authority and, in the immediate postwar years took it upon itself to draft a blacklist and organize the trials that would punish collaborationist writers and intellectuals. Paulhan became increasingly frustrated by the Céné's positions, refused to sign the blacklist, and ultimately offered his resignation in protest. He was openly critical of the Céné's so-called *épuration* of literature, and, after his resignation, was accused by some of having betrayed the cause. The controversies went on for many years, and by 1952, Paulhan took the position of condemning the purges in their totality, as he does here in his "Letter to the Directors of the Resistance," a letter addressed to old friends who have declared themselves sole "directors" of the Resistance's legacy. For a related discussion, see Jean Paulhan, *De la paille et du grain* (Paris: Gallimard, 1948), available in English as *Of Chaff and Wheat:*

Writers, War, and Treason, trans. and with an introduction by Richard Rand (Urbana: University of Illinois Press, 2004).

The "Letter to the Directors of the Resistance" was first published in book form by Éditions de Minuit in 1952, and, once again, Paulhan was publicly attacked by his former colleagues. His vigorous replies were published and appended to the original letter in a subsequent edition (Paris: Jean-Jacques Pauvert, 1968). The complete text is included in the *Œuvres complètes,* volume 5, pp. 429–42.

LETTER TO THE DIRECTORS OF THE RESISTANCE

Translated by Charlotte Mandell

Gentlemen:

I am a Resistant. I began being one in June '40, and I am one still, or at least I think of myself as one. But I no longer take any pride in it. Shame, instead. Every day I see that resisting was not as simple as it first seemed. But let me start from the beginning.

Whoever entered the Resistance immediately felt better. What he was doing seemed to him a good thing. He became a kind of hero, who was just as worthy as a military hero (without the bother of the uniform and the knapsack—especially not the knapsack!). Of course he was risking death—but still, he told himself, there wasn't much chance of that. Failing death, there were prison and exile—but they would come to an end, he told himself, on the day of Victory (since he believed in this Victory; and no one knew yet about the ignominy of the concentration camps). In any case, he was on the right side, once and for all: the side of Justice and Right. This is something that helps you live and die.

Yes, that's what the Resistant thought (though not as clearly). And, of course, he was mistaken. What he was risking was quite different; in one sense, it was much worse: every day he risked becoming the opposite of a hero—scum, and even the lowest sort of scum. He risked betraying his friends. Everything depended on how he resisted torture. I don't even mean the pain, which it is possible to bear. But the terrifying feeling that torture, by letting you live, will damage you forever, will leave you with nothing but a dislocated body, an imbecilic mind. So his first decision forced him to make other decisions (much more serious). His courage forced him to undertake other kinds of courage (much more heroic). Far from being righteous all his life, he took the infinite risk of becoming unrighteous: of finding he had become, overnight, a swine.

It's these kinds of things that make us say life is unfair. It is possible. Let this serve as a warning to anyone who wants to take the path of virtue.

I will come back to that. In any case, what I have to say isn't cheerful either. I'd much rather not have to say it. But since none of us is saying it, I'll have to say it. It is the Resistants I'm addressing. I'll take the liberty of telling them they've fallen into the trap: they are just as cowardly or traitorous, just as unjust as one of them who betrayed his comrades on the torture rack. (But with fewer excuses.)

SCORNING THE LAW

A declaration should be fairly made, before any discussion, about what we propose to establish and what we will set aside. Well, I will not pose the slightest political or social question. That is not my business. It will not be a question here of fascism or democracy. Nor will I try to establish whether Pétain was or was not a traitor; if Brasillach deserved death; if Maurras was guilty of sharing intelligence with the enemy. All I propose to say is that Maurras, Brasillach, and Pétain have never been *judged*. They are not one among the 400,000 French[1] who, after the Liberation, were executed, sentenced to hard labor, fired, ruined, accused of being a national disgrace, and reduced to the rank of pariah—of all those French, every one of them has been struck without any regard whatsoever for Law and Justice. I will begin with the Law.

I am not an enemy of Codes, or of Logic or Grammar books. I have always thought there was more mischievousness, and even genius, in these old books than is usually thought. I don't always have the patience to check them to see. However, I know of a Chinese treatise from the fifth century B.C. that denounces precisely the odd quirks of lettrism. And if little Saillet had read Aristotle's *Rhetoric*, he would never have mistaken an exercise by Mlle. Akakia for an unpublished poem of Rimbaud.[2]

I was not too surprised, then, to hear Magistrates and Ministers declare, after the Liberation, that it was enough, in order to punish justly all the traitors and those who denounced Resistants, those who helped to create or profited from Collaboration, to open the Penal Code to Article 75. Fine. That the judges were to be inspired only by a scrupulous legality. So be it. Moreover, that a criminal never invented anything. And so on.[3]

In the end, it was almost too beautiful. It made one yearn to go see the thing itself.

So I went and looked.

It's a little long, this Article 75 in question. A little long, but fiendishly precise. None of those perplexing words that ministers and attorneys general exploit, which can mean whatever you like: *honor, dignity, courage, moral unity, freedom.* In point of fact, the word *collaboration* doesn't appear even once. But terms as simple as *bear arms* (against France), *hand over to the foreigner supplies, weapons, arsenals, munitions, buildings, material, cities, fortresses, territories* (belonging to France), *making enlistments* (in the service of a foreign power at war with France), *sharing intelligence* (with an enemy of France). All that amounts to treason, which is punishable, in principle, by death.[4]

Yes, all these words are simple, and easy to define. With the exception of one single word, though, that turns up in every sentence. It is, as often happens, the one whose meaning seems, at first glance, the most obvious: *France.*

What is France? Of course, it is not a question here of a country in the sense of geography (mountains and streams couldn't care less if they were betrayed). Or of a pretty girl with a Phrygian bonnet (no, no more than England is a lion, or the United States an uncle). Nor is it a question—in any case, it is not just a question—of the eldest daughter of the Church (according to Massillon). Nor of the Christ among the Nations (according to Quinet). Nor of the Paradise of Initiative (according to Maurras). Nor of the France of the Revolution (or the France of the kings). France, in short, is no less difficult to define than man.

But I'll go back to my Code. It doesn't hesitate for an instant. As soon as it has to specify the detail and degree of the treasons or, better, the "attacks on the exterior security of the State": he is guilty (it says) who bears arms . . . *without having been approved by the Government;* who hands over . . . *without Government authorization;* who enlists . . . *scorning the prohibitions decreed by the Government;* who shares intelligence . . .

without the permission of the Government. And that is very clear. It is not a question of an ideal; or of a symbol; or even of a country or a nation. It is precisely a question of the Government this nation has given itself (or at least that it supports); and the decisions of this Government. I do not know if M. Daladier did well to declare war on Germany in '39. I do not know at all if Messieurs Pleven and Queuille are right to continue the Vietnam war. But from the instant they did so, I betray—not M. Pleven or M. Daladier, but France; I am precisely a traitor, and punishable by death, if I happen to hand over to Hitler or to the Viet-minh the map of a fort, an aerodrome, a simple little rifle. That is what is very clear, and I am warned. In short, France—this France one can betray—is such as has been defined by the legal Government of the moment. That is the point of view of the Code, and I do not deny that it is a little simplistic. (But at the moment it is only a question of law.)

That said, one single question poses itself: From '40 to '44, what *was* the legal Government of France? Here—everyone will agree, alas!—there is no place for the slightest doubt. Yes, the Belgian Ministry was in London, yes, the Dutch Government was in London, but the French Government was in Vichy. And the ambassadors to France from the United States, Russia, the Vatican, were in Vichy. Never did General de Gaulle speak of *his* government;[5] never did he retain by force—as his first duty would have been, if he had represented France—a single French soldier passing through London. On August 16, '44, Édouard Herriot, addressing Pierre Laval, still calls him "Monsieur le Chef du Gouvernement." Édouard Herriot is in the business—he knows what he's saying. And we other Resistants weren't the least bit governmental, nor were we decent, obedient citizens. We were conscientious objectors and rebels. We appealed against Vichy—and against the definition Vichy gave of France—toward a more courageous, more righteous France. Doing that seemed to us to redeem all at once the stupid and cowardly acts of our ministers after the Armistice—not even the Armistice of '40, but the old one, of '18. That is what we said, as best we could, in our little clandestine newspapers.

For we had no *Journal officiel*, it goes without saying. But Vichy's *Journal officiel* told us, one day, that M. Paul Reynaud, and M. Vincent Auriol the next day, and the day after that Messieurs Léon Blum, Jules Moch, and Édouard Herriot, meant to place all power in the hands of Marshal Pétain—who was urged, moreover, to negotiate, to come to an agreement—in short, to collaborate—with Germany. This was ratified on July 10 by the National Assembly. (De Gaulle's summons was on June 18.)

The Code, then, to whomever questions it, clearly responds: one single Government, that of Marshal Pétain, was qualified to judge the treasons committed—in the Occupied Zone, for instance—between '40 and '44. And it was to that government you had first to appeal. Even if it meant judging it later on in turn.[6]

AGAINST ALL JUSTICE

I'll make a special effort to demonstrate the evidence. Let's imagine that a coup had replaced Daladier with a fascist minister, on January 1, '40. Do you think the new Government would have had the *right*—I mean the *legal* right—once peace with Germany had been concluded, to throw anyone into prison? To execute the officers and soldiers who had marched off to war under the orders of the radical minister? Really! Are you going to tell me there are treasons that go unnoticed at the time? What a joke! What you are prosecuting (you say) are public treasons: newspaper articles, radio talks, speeches. . . .

"Unnoticed," you add, "by their perpetrators themselves." Here you're speaking of blindness, cowardliness, stupidity—obstinate mistakes, wicked mistakes, and grave ones.[7] But I have to stop you right there. In vain do I examine and re-examine my Code; I can't find one single article that punishes mistakes, stupidity, or cowardliness.

Then will you say to me, "Liberation was a Revolution"? If it's a Revolution, let it create its own language, invent its own laws![8] Let it even decide—against the oldest principles of Law—that its edicts will have a retroactive effect! Force has the rights of force. It debases itself and humiliates itself—and humiliates us all—as soon as it lies, and covers its assassinations with a legal cloak. (For I finally find that also in my Code: that an execution contravening the law is called a murder.)

"If we are to understand you correctly, then, there are no guilty men?" Oh, but yes there are! And who sometimes deserved a more rigorous justice. Or in any case an authentic justice.

You'll say to me finally: "Well then, they weren't the only ones." Of course not. They would join the sixty thousand or so Frenchmen who were tortured, shot, or burned alive by the Liberation.[9] True. But that was without any trial. But each one of us could say as an honest Resistant: "I didn't want that to happen. It was foreign groups that did all that. It was

Communist cells. . . ." This time, you can't say that. You're the ones who have cheated. And what cheating it is, that creates 340,000 victims!

To tell the truth, only one question can be asked here: how is it that your lie was accepted so easily? How is it that you weren't the first ones to be embarrassed, harassed, frightened? Here's what I imagine, quite haphazardly, to be your excuse: that an illusion must have been in play, crude but seductive, one we could call: *prediction of the past.*

It seems to us after the fact, when an event has occurred, that we were expecting it and were confusedly preparing for it. This seems even truer when it happens to someone else. We see this headline in the papers: "Murder for 100 francs," which implies, more or less vaguely, that the murderer had foreseen the one hundred francs, that he committed his crime *all the same.* (But if he'd found one hundred thousand francs, do you think he'd have left them there?) The word *end* signifies *intention* no less than *conclusion,* and it's hardly surprising that we tend to confuse one meaning with the other. When all is said and done, the condemnation of Maurras (among others) to death can only be explained—I am not saying "can only be justified"—if we obscurely acknowledge that Maurras, as early as 1940, foreseeing the Liberation, opposed this Liberation in advance—opposed the new face it was going to give France—out of pure perfidy: out of sheer devilishness. Or: that he had always been opposed to it, even before the wars. . . .

But I suppose that the role of the Codes, or in any case the role of the magistrates, is precisely to defend us against such base and seemingly childish illusions.

Put aside the Codes and judges, people will tell me. So much the better that France has shaken off this dust! It's justice I hunger and thirst for, not legality. It's all those notions, the name for which doesn't appear in your Dalloz: honor and dignity, liberty, the rights of man. Your Pétain may well have been legal, but he was not legitimate. Precisely. I'm coming to that.

It is all too true that the same distance, or close to it, exists between Law and Justice as between the letter and the spirit: the letter, always ready to encroach on the spirit, to restrain it and diminish it—always ready to become a dead letter. But the spirit is hardy and free, able to escape the traps of automatism, and to be reborn at any instant. Yes, I know all that, and it is no doubt a fact—just as there exist alongside writers who are minutely concerned with rules and emendation, other writers given entirely over to their inspiration, their madness, alone—that one finds, opposite magistrates devoted to the law, jurors who are simply concerned with justice and liberty, honor, truth. And of course in the case in question they scarcely showed themselves to be men of law; they seemed to be so only at the price of an abuse of authority. But these jurors . . .

With these jurors, everything was strangely arranged as if to protect them at all cost from any sense of and taste for—from any temptation to—Justice. To force them to choose murder.

We know how the juries of the justice courts were recruited: from among those French who had resisted the occupier with all their soul and strength. From among them, those who had suffered most, in their bodies, or in their loss of property: unjustly imprisoned, stripped bare, tortured, deported with their parents and children. At first sight, that seems an excellent decision. And who really could have known better than we Resistants the intentions or wishes of a new France—of the France we were going to create. It would have been much too unfair to give the floor—and the authority—just after such a tragedy, to the ones who had stayed cowardly at home and cared only about their own little affairs (more often than not, going along with the enemy): to the ones who hadn't taken sides. On the contrary, the care of Justice was going to be entrusted to men who had *gone through it;* in a way, to specialists in the matter; to those who knew exactly what was at stake. And this something was always torture and despoiling, humiliations and crimes.

The intention, of course, seems fair at first sight. It is wise, it is eminently reasonable. What would be more absurd than electing juries to judge theft or murder in a haphazard fashion, juries possibly closed off from all moral concerns—who knows, they themselves might be guilty (at least in thought) of various crimes. They were going to change all that. Who better to judge a theft, after all, than a jury of people who had been robbed? An adultery, than a jury of cuckolds? A killer, than a victim? They're the ones who would understand the matter. Who would be in touch! Whom lawyers wouldn't befuddle. After all, a theft, a murder, even a treason, doesn't necessarily succeed the first time; and if it were enough to rid oneself of a few moral principles, the thing would be much too easy. One wouldn't earn the slightest merit by doing so. No, it is an undertaking that assumes (especially when repeated), aside from passion, some science, organization, a hint of method. What could be fairer than forming, to judge a technique, a jury of technicians? But I'll come back to that.

DISDAINING FAIRNESS

Every day we hear this, and each of us has thought it (or at least felt moved to think it) a thousand times: "Spare me your generalities, your metaphysics. My feet are planted firmly on the ground. I know (pretty well) where my interests, my enjoyments lie. I have a wife and children. What do I have to do with your dialectics, with your thesis and antithesis, with your identity of contraries (or contrariness of identities)? Enough hot air!"

Yes. But listen to what you are saying, look at yourself a little for five minutes. You just wanted gently to convince a friend, give a lesson to your son. But as soon as they resist you, it's because they're deliberately trying (you say) not to understand. So you feel irritation overcoming you, already you're clenching your fists. Your wife, though! For her you have nothing but love. Of course. But if you ever suspect her of lying to you, though—of having lied to you from the beginning—you see red. Already you imagine her dead, not without pleasure. Now go be surprised that governments, the better to defend freedom, begin by suppressing it; the better to establish peace, they begin by waging war, and decide so quickly to annihilate those they don't think they can convince. Go be surprised. . . .

For instance, that our collaborators did not encounter enemies who were more determined—more courageous too (during the times when courage was still an issue)—than *other* collaborators. Who of course refused to collaborate with Germany; but that was because—they told us this very clearly, they kept repeating it in every possible way—because they had chosen another collaboration. They had no wish whatever to come to an agreement with Germany: no, they wanted to come to an agreement with Russia. Thus these extremes met. These contraries were contraries only because they so resembled each other: both sides of course focused on ensuring a lasting public happiness—whether by means of the triumph of a class too long oppressed (according to the Communists), or of a race too long downtrodden (according to the fascists). They had decided once and for all: both kinds of triumph seemed to them faithful (they said) to the sense of history. They even called the wars they still had to wage "peace." For each problem, they had a solution. Sometimes the solution even preceded the problem. (Thus remedies are being discovered today although no one yet knows what illness they might cure.) They also took the side of the poor against the rich, and of proletarian nations against prosperous governments. And they were ready to sacrifice their peace and their lives (or even better, the lives of others) for the triumph of their doctrine. They were convinced in any case that such an end justified the means: informing and treason, corruption, torture, and capital punishment daily, concentration camps and forced labor, a subservient press, state-monitored literature, the deification of a leader, the enslavement of conquered races (or classes). In short, the Reign of Terror, with all the fear, but also fascination that implies—with all the cruelty, but also all the appeal.

I am stating the facts. I am not trying to judge anyone. They were upstanding and firm and eager to shed their blood! They resembled each other even in their impatience. Perhaps these (if I may say so) bore an even greater resemblance than the others. Indeed, *Les Lettres françaises* corresponds precisely to *Je suis partout; La Nouvelle Critique* to *Combat.*[10] The arguments are the same, it's the same enthusiasm. Sometimes it's even the same writers, who have changed their targets, but not their subjects or their methods. It's the same huge party that follows them and in its turn wants to think only through them. A party that may be vaster than it's ever been: treason in France has always seemed distinguished; today it is popular without ceasing to be elegant, and society people who crowd around the Céné sales may chance to encounter some petty clerk or proletarian there.[11] It may simply seem, no doubt thanks to this popularity, that the Châteaubriants and Brasillachs of today—an Aragon, an Eluard, a Claude Morgan—more openly show their desire to collaborate, that they have more carefully calculated the ways and means. If they speak of peace, of the sense of history and the rest, they do so (seemingly) with a little more science and conviction.

You'll say to me, then, that they haven't had the chance, at least not until now, to carry out their intentions, and that the Law regards as innocent every criminal who hasn't begun to carry out his crime—even if the poison is already poured out, and the trap set. That may be true for the Law. But it's Justice that we're talking about. I'll come back to that. It is to these (virtual)[12] collaborators that the task has been entrusted of judging the (perfectly real) collaborators France has accused. In fact, Communists made up the majority in most of the law courts. Even when they didn't make up the majority, they were the ones who gained authority over the others, and imposed their points of view; they were the ones with demands. For this to come about (as well as for the appointment of the juries of Resistants) there was no need for a particular decree.[13] No. It was done, so to speak, all by itself. First of all, the Communists wanted so very much to be jurors that people let them. Because it is hard to find jurors. The average Frenchman—even if he is a Resistant—hardly likes to work all day for a meager fee. He would rather call in sick. And then, he might have said to himself that the Communist tenacity during the Resistance really did deserve some reward—a kind of compensation.

And why not? you'll say.

Why not, in fact? I said just now that one could easily imagine a jury of people who had been robbed, to judge a thief; or a jury of victims, to judge a killer. No doubt. But it is possible to go even further in this direction. (And we have actually gone there.) To empanel actual juries not from victims of the technique, but from technicians. (And they have been formed.) In short, to summon a jury of thieves (all established, experienced) to judge a thief; a jury of murderers (preferably retired ones) to judge a murderer; a jury of collaborators to judge a collaborator. (That is precisely what they have done.) They would be in the know, the ones that no one had managed to put away. Real specialists. I have seen these juries! They were a brave sight. They moved like columns. Often the most honest, upright people in the world. But they knew they were there to condemn. The Party had told them so. The Republic seemed to repeat it to them. They condemned. With all their might. They were unyielding. But were they just?

As it happens it's easy to find out. Almost too easy. A sort of grammar of ideas is in play here that is neither less apt nor less decisive than our grammar of words (that spontaneous grammar that startles us, or makes us break out laughing before an ill-constructed sentence, a word pronounced the wrong way). And it is, after all, the ensemble of reactions of this other grammar that is called "justice." Thus, Justice or the grammar in question states that it is good—that it is inevitable—to consult a technician whenever it's a matter of finding out if the victim was indeed poisoned (and by what poison), if the banknotes were real or bogus, and if the plans of the fortress or airplane hangar were indeed genuine plans—if the collaboration was a real collaboration—and what article of the Code deals with the crime committed. Yes, but when it is a question of finding out *who* the poisoner, or the forger, or the collaborator, is, and if he deserves mercy or not, the technician is put aside and we summon the opposite of the technician: the ignoramus, the common man—who has never yet been poisoned, and has never poisoned anyone; who has not been a victim of collaborators and has no intention of becoming a collaborator himself; who is prejudiced neither for nor against. In short, the man who has nothing to do with any of it. And that's even the best definition one can give of democracy—in the sense that we are all democrats. As long as it's a matter of actions that are a little extraordinary, like making a watch, drawing up a marriage contract, or building a court of justice, only the specialist will do: the architect, the notary public, the watchmaker. Yes, but as soon as it's a matter of telling the time, of falling in love, or of meting out the Justice that is (or should be) in the court, well then, we're all equally qualified. And it can even happen—in love, for instance—that the most ignorant of us gets on better than the professional.

What a strange trust is thus confided (you will say) to the first to come along, to anyone at all! But under the names of "Christianity," "humanity," "the rights of man," "freedom" or "democracy," it is the basis of our old world. In short, Justice has been no less betrayed in the circumstances than the Law. There is not one political prisoner who has been condemned—not one of your victims—in whom I can't see the terrifying image of judicial error.

At this some point some idiot will say to me: "Don't pretend to be so innocent. Why do you refuse to see the politics of the thing? War and occupation in our time have ceased to be national. . . ."

"But I was always told that the wars of the Revolution were wars of ideas. And what about the Crusades? And the Napoleonic Wars? And the Trojan War. . . ."

"They became political (our idiot continues), and the justice that comes after them is political too. If your four hundred thousand new friends have been struck down, it's not because they helped Germany. It's because they opposed the forward march of progress: they opposed history itself."

"Oh, but that's different. Are you telling me it was for fascism that you condemned Pétain? And Maurras for monarchism? And Béraud, I suppose, for Anglophobia? Well then, stop lying. Confess it, once and for all. And I will write you a second letter."

Let's leave all those people, and they are countless, who wouldn't sacrifice the nail of their little finger for Peace, not one hair of their filthy heads for Justice. It's the others I am speaking to.

Above all to the Resistants. Can't they see they've been caught in a trap? That they thought they were Resistant once and for all: pure, saved. But now they have fallen lower than the very people they have condemned? No, they were so proud of having one day found themselves on the right side that they all became moralists. Vercors has stopped showing us those cynical sketches, at which he excelled: he weighs, feels, palpates, cases of conscience. Aragon, Eluard have left off extolling the merits of abortion, crime, and defeatism: now they sing in one voice of hope, the joy of living, and large families. Sartre is perfecting, not without honest efforts, an Ethics. In the meantime he has founded a journal, which pursues injustice far and wide. We know he has already found seven hundred little motes in Stalin's eye, and twelve thousand in Truman's. For Franco, they can't even be counted anymore. It is time, it is high time, they started attending to the beam in their own eyes.

Then there are the Christians among you. There are even people who live on Justice and Truth: there are rabbis, ministers, priests. Strange priests, though. Strange ministers. Strange rabbis. What are they waiting for? Why don't they say we have been tricked for seven years? Why don't they shout it from the rooftops?

But what can we do? They ask. I know nothing about that. I am not a politician or a judge. Nor am I a priest. All I can see—but I can see it clearly—is that horror and disgust will awaken us tomorrow if we close our eyes today. We have coming to us certain arrears of justice and of right. Let us have it! And then, it must be possible, let them keep us well-informed.

That is all I wanted to say to you. *Salut et Fraternité.*

NOTES

The Experience of the Proverb

1. The *filanjana* is a kind of sedan chair.

2. The long horns of these little clay bulls sculpted by Malagasy children are the most delicate part. The proverb's meaning is, roughly: every clay bull will lose its horns eventually.

3. A little girl's name.

4. It is too late to talk to her.

5. The "wagging tongue" is already going around repeating: "How dusty it is at Ranona's! How filthy!"

6. The poor man, chatting with his wealthy neighbor, did not have time to collect wood. When he gets home, he has no choice but to use his door to start his fire.

7. [I have not been able to locate this passage in Swift. The translation, therefore, is mine.—Trans.]

8. ["*Tant va la cruche à l'eau qu'à la fin elle se casse.*" This French proverb has no ready translation in English, but the old jug is roughly the equivalent of the proverbial straw that breaks the camel's back.—Trans.]

Jacob Cow the Pirate, or, If Words Are Signs

1. In 1917.

2. [The passage plays on a common French saying: "If Cleopatra's nose had been shorter, the face of the earth would have been forever changed."—Trans.]

3. [I cite Paul Knight's translations of Lautréamont's *Poésies*, from Comte de Lautréamont, *Maldoror and Poems*, trans. Paul Knight (London: Penguin, 1978), 268–70, 273. Lautréamont's maxims frequently reproduce Pascal's *Pensées*, in some cases verbatim. Paulhan seems to allude to this fact in the next paragraph.—Trans.]

4. [The pun in the original depends on the homonymy of two French words:

les menuisers, which are cabinet makers or joiners, and *nuire,* which means to injure, discredit, or otherwise do harm.—Trans.]

5. [*Traire,* which in modern usage means "to milk" (an animal), is related etymologically to the verb *tirer,* which means "to pull," "drag," "draw," as well as, in the case of an image, "to print," "strike," "pull," or "run off" multiple copies (as with a press).—Trans.]

6. [*Belette* means "weasel" but suggests a diminutive form of the noun *belle,* or "pretty thing."—Trans.]

7. [All of the "metaphors" in this paragraph appeal to images or etymologies that are either false or lost. Thus *accoster* means to "berth" a vessel, *aborder* means to "board" or "ram" a vessel (in the course of an attack), and *échouer* means to "beach" or "run (a vessel) aground." The horse evokes an apocryphal relation between *travail,* to "work," and the verb *entraver,* which means to "fetter" or "shackle."—Trans.]

Rhetoric Rises from Its Ashes

1. ["*Les lieux*" is a term of ancient rhetoric that can be translated either as "topic" or as "commonplace." The *Oxford English Dictionary* defines the "common place" in its ancient sense as "A passage of general application, such as may serve as the basis of argument; a leading text cited in argument."—Trans.]

2. Victor Hugo. [I quote George S. Burleigh's 1867 translation of *La Légende des siècles.*—Trans.]

3. Jean-Baptiste Massillon.

4. [*Louer* can be both to let or rent and to praise or laud, as the Latin etyma suggest.—Trans.]

Young Lady with Mirrors

1. See "Rhetoric Rises from Its Ashes," in this volume.

2. Whence *l'ance* or *lance* (see also *hedera-lierre*); and the suffixes *quin, quine* (see also *rouquin* [redhead], etc.).

3. Villon.

4. *Quelques livres. Œuvres,* vol. III.

5. *Mme. Dacier et les traductions d'Homère.*

Key to Poetry

1. [For the opposition between Terror and Rhetoric, see Paulhan's *Les Fleurs de Tarbes, ou, La Terreur dans les lettres* (Paris: Gallimard, 1941); *The Flowers of Tarbes, or, Terror in Literature,* trans. Michael Syrotinski (Urbana: University of Illinois Press, 2005). See also "Rhetoric Rises from Its Ashes" and "Young Lady with Mirrors,"in this volume.—Trans.]

2. The reader will have recognized Rimbaud, Moréas, Gourmont, and Chateaubriand.

3. ["Qu'avez-vous?" can mean all of these things in French: "What is ailing you?" but also, "What do you have to declare?"—Trans.]

4. See p. 131: "By *law* I mean the regularly occurring relation we may observe or produce between two facts. . . ."; p. 135: "The poets are my first witnesses. Dangerous witnesses, to be sure, and partial, naturally tendentious, not a little biased. . . ."; p. 138: "The subject they deal with—expression—seems more established, more clearly delimited. . . ."

5. In his book, strangely entitled *La Pensée et la langue,* Ferdinand Brunot seeks only to lay out the grammar of French as it is used, and not at all to extract, from the relations between thought and language, the least general law.

6. Saussure, *Cours de linguistique générale,* p. 162. [See also Saussure, *Cours de linguistique générale* (Paris: Payot, 1995), p. 155. In the case of both Saussure and Bally, Paulhan gives page references to editions unknown. It should also be noted that his quotations are not always accurate and frequently abridge or reverse the order of sentences. In quoting Saussure, I have consulted the translation published in *Course in General Linguistics,* ed. Charles Bally, Albert Sechehaye, and Albert Riedlinger, trans. Wade Baskin (New York: McGraw-Hill, 1966 [1959]) and silently modified it where necessary. As above, I have also given page references, in brackets in the endnotes, to the most widely available French edition of the Saussure.—Trans.]

7. Bally, *Stylistique française,* p. 87.

8. Bally, p. 176.

9. Saussure, p. 185 [p. 179.—Trans.].

10. Bally, p. 22.

11. Bally, p. 187.

12. Bally, p. 195.

13. Bally, p. 258.

14. Bally, p. 258.

15. Bally, p. 171.

16. Bally, p. 14.

17. Bally, p. 100.

18. Bally, *Linguistique générale et linguistique française,* p. 289. "A wolf is a woeful thing for sheep in the fold."

19. *Linguistique générale et linguistique française,* p. 289.

20. Brunot makes the same mistake when he distinguishes between temporal verbs, negative verbs, verbs of measure, locative verbs, verbs of manner, verbs of matter, etc. Or between the different grammatical complements of intention, exchange, relation, purpose, and result.

21. See p. 139: " It sometimes happens that the same treatment is suggested in both registers. . . ."; p. 140: "The reflections carried out by Baudelaire and Shelley,

Lamartine and Mallarmé have nothing in common—not even the language they use . . ."; pp. 147–48: "I would have to admit [. . .] that every image is a function of words, but at the same time a group of thoughts. . . ."

22. [The following quotations attributed to André Breton are taken (although Paulhan indicates this only at this first occurrence) from the *Manifesto of Surrealism* of 1924 and *Soluble Fish.* Unless otherwise indicated, translations are from André Breton, *Manifestoes of Surrealism*, trans. Richard Seaver and Helen R. Lane (Ann Arbor: University of Michigan Press, 1972).—Trans.]

23. *La jeune génération littéraire* (*Le Navire d'argent*). [My translation. *Le Navire d'argent* was a monthly literary publication edited by Adrienne Monnier in Paris in the years 1925 and 1926.—Trans.]

24. [The first two quotes are from *Soluble Fish* (*Op.cit.*, pp. 54–55 and 51); the third is from the *Manifesto of Surrealism* (*Op. cit.*, p. 38).—Trans.]

25. [*Manifesto of Surrealism,* p. 39.—Trans.]

26. [The first sentence here ("Experience [. . .] to make it emerge") is from the *Manifesto,* p. 10. The others could not be located (the translations are therefore mine).—Trans.]

27. [The pun here, with "broyé" and "noirci" (broyer du noir: to brood or be down in the dumps) is lost in translation.—Trans.]

28. [Here again Paulhan quotes Breton a little carelessly. The first sentence appears on p. 36 of the *Manifesto,* but "they come to him spontaneously, despotically. He cannot chase them away" is in fact Breton quoting Baudelaire.—Trans.]

29. [The first sentence (like the second, already quoted once) is taken from Breton's *Manifesto,* p. 39. The third is from *Soluble Fish,* p. 73.—Trans.]

30. [Paulhan seems to be rewriting, in his own words, a famous passage taken from the *Manifesto,* p. 36. This is therefore my translation.—Trans.]

31. *Le Temps,* July 25, 1925.

32. *Les Nouvelles littéraires,* March 3, 1925.

33. See p. 160: "If the strict and simple observers of language fall into the same trap awaiting the doctrinarians of poetry, and are overtaken by the event in the same way, this means the same event that makes poetry was already at work in the simplest expression"; p. 138: "Thus one suspects that the key, once discovered, would also be valid for domains other than literature or poetry"; p. 133: "For poetry to be, it is necessary—but it seems to be enough—that there be communication, conversation, some intercourse."

34. [From Racine's *Phedra,* famously pronounced by Théophile Gautier the most beautiful line of poetry in the French language.—Trans.]

Democracy Calls on the First to Come Along

1. [*La démocratie fait appel au premier venu:* the title and related phrases pose several obstacles to translation. First is the semantic reach of the French

phrase "*faire appel*," which includes the more formal or juridical senses of "to appeal" or "make an appeal" while nonetheless retaining the more colloquial senses of a call, request, or demand. Thus democracy might be understood to "appeal to" or "make an appeal to" something or someone, but also simply to "call on" or "out (to)" him. This person poses his (her?) own set of problems. I have rendered "*le premier venu*" as "the first to come along." Among the other translations one could also give are "anyone you like," "any old person," or even "anyone whatsoever." Also worth noting is that "*le premier venu*" is much more common in French than any one of these phrases in English.—Trans.]

The Bee

1. [The phrase here, "*peu de chose*," loses nuance in translation. "It's no big thing," one might say today in English; the dictionaries say, "*une petite chose*," "*quelque chose d'insignifiant*," meaning, roughly, "the littlest thing," "a trifle," with the most colloquial translations tending toward an outright negation: "It's nothing," "That makes no difference," "It doesn't matter."—Trans.]

Letter on Peace

1. [*Le Rassemblement démocratique révolutionnaire* (Democratic Revolutionary Union), a coalition of different groups from the Left, was cofounded by Sartre in 1948 and disbanded shortly thereafter.—Trans.]

Letter to the Directors about Europe

1. [André Philip was the French minister of economy in the successive governments of Gouin, Blu, and Ramadier after World War II. He was a fervent militant of the construction of Europe (and the author of *L'Europe unie* and other books). Paul Henri Spaak, a Belgian foreign minister, was the first elected president of the General Assembly of the United Nations, and president of the Council of Europe from 1949 to 1951. He was also actively engaged in the construction of a supranational Europe.—Trans.]

2. See the "Letter on Peace," in this volume.

Letter to the Directors of the Resistance

1. This number is, in all likelihood, less than the actual number. It is currently acknowledged that one million French were arrested at the Liberation (see also *Le Figaro*, April 6, 1946), and more than sixty thousand of them were executed. Furthermore, official statistics indicate that in 1948, there were ninety thousand condemnations issued by the civil and criminal courts. Administrative purging

affected more than 120,000 officers, judges, and functionaries. Professional, political, union, or journalistic purging, about three hundred thousand (see also *Report to the U.N.* by the Union for Restoration of the Public Service, 1951). If you consider, while pondering this, that a man killed, or merely dishonored, involves the ruin of his entire family, you quickly arrive at one and a half million victims.

2. [In 1949, *Le Mercure de France* published the poem "La Chasse spirituelle," enthusiastically prefaced by Pascal Pia. It was said to be the long-lost manuscript of a Rimbaud poem left behind by Verlaine when he abandoned his wife and child. Over the years, the lost poem had become an obsession among specialists of Rimbaud's work, and its publication plunged the world of letters into turmoil. André Breton was quick, however, to recognize "La Chasse spirituelle" for what it really was: a hoax, a clever pastiche written by Nicolas Bataille and Mlle Akakia-Viala.—Trans.]

3. I quote our ministers of justice: Messieurs Teitgen, de Menthon, André Marie; the General Prosecutor Boissarie: "The purging had only to be founded on the traditional principles of our Codes, applied in full and scrupulous legality" (*Réquisitoire contre J.-H. Paquis*).

4. Here is the text of the article in question (see also Dalloz, pp. 92–93): "Art. 75. Will be guilty of treason, and punishable by death:

1. Any Frenchman who bears arms against France;
2. Any Frenchman who shares intelligence with a foreign power, with the aim of involving it in undertaking hostilities against France, or provides it with the means, either by facilitating the penetration of foreign forces into French territory, or by undermining the loyalty of the armies of land, sea, or air, or in any other manner;
3. Any Frenchman who hands over to a foreign power or its agents, either French troops, or territories, cities, fortresses, structures, posts, stores, weapons arsenals, materials, munitions, ships, buildings, or aerial navigation systems, belonging to France, or to countries over which the authority of France is exercised;
4. Any Frenchman who, in wartime, provokes soldiers or marines to enter the service of a foreign power, facilitates the means for them to do so, or makes enlistments for a foreign power at war with France;
5. Any Frenchman who, in wartime, shares intelligence with a foreign power, or with its agents, with the aim of favoring the enterprises of this power against France.

Those persons will be considered French, in the sense of the present section, who are native to countries over which the authority of France is exercised, as well as foreign soldiers or marines serving France.

That territory will be considered French, in the sense of the present section, the territory of countries over which the authority of France is exercised.

5. Quite the contrary. He said clearly and frankly, in his speech on April 2, 1941: "We do not want to modify French institutions. Thus we do not deem it necessary to take the title of 'government' to exercise the authority we need."

6. The excellent writer who gives his signature to *Servus juris* fortuitously outlined this question in his *Open Letter to Messieurs the Presidents of the Courts of Justice* (André Bonne, 1948).

7. See "These 150,000 collaborators, from whom explanations had to be requested, are not 150,000 traitors, deserving death. Among them, there are abominable traitors—we'll say a few hundred. Then there are despicable cowards, then half-cowards, equally despicable; finally there are a lot of imbeciles." (P.-H. Teitgen, minister of justice. See also *L'Officiel*, meeting of August 6, 1946.) See also: "I will not, I think, need to insist to persuade you of my profound desire not to let the heads be raised again of those men who, for months on end, delighted in criminal error" (André Marie, Minister of Justice. *L'Officiel*, March 19, 1948).

8. As was done in Nuremberg.

9. Current estimations vary between sixty thousand and two hundred thousand dead. According to the only official document we have, the reports of the Historical Section of Eisenhower's administration, there were about fifty thousand victims for the Mediterranean region alone. (See also the *American Mercury*, April 1946.)

Adrien Tixier, minister of the interior, in 1945, estimated the number of summary executions at 105,000 between June 1944 and February 1945. (See also the letter from Colonel Dewawrin, quoted by Jean Bernier, *Le Crapouillot*, No. 11.)

10. Here, of course, I am referring to the *Combat* of 1937–39.

11. [The "Céné," or the *Comité National des Écrivains*, was founded in 1943, in secrecy, under the German occupation, by writers who were members of the Resistance (many of them had close ties to the PCF, or Parti Communiste Français). Paulhan was a founding member. The CNE or Céné quickly established itself, after the Liberation, as a *tribunal des lettres*, issuing a blacklist of writers who had disgraced themselves by being collaborators, and calling for purges among writers. Paulhan, as early as September 1944, had second thoughts, denounced the blacklist, and opposed the leading members of the CNE, in many cases, the very people he addresses here (still, five years later) as the directors of the Resistance. Popular sales of books, similar to book fairs, were organized by the Céné each year, with many of the writers present. For detailed accounts of Paulhan's participation in the Céné and of his role in the literary and publishing arms of the Resistance more generally, see Richard Rand's introduction to Jean Paulhan, *Of Chaff and Wheat: Writers, War, and Treason*, as noted in our own introduction.—Trans.]

12. Not so virtual, really. Think of the events of 1939–41, of the desertion of Maurice Thorez, and the rest.

13. It is fair to note here that this decree was added, and was to go in effect as of January 1, 1947, when sixty-four law courts—out of eighty-nine—had already completed their trials, and when only little affairs were left to the other courts. As to recommencing the trials whose illegality was thus recognized, the question has never been raised.

INDEX

JEAN PAULHAN (1884–1968) is often referred to as the "grey eminence" of the publishing world in France, where he played a central role in literary and intellectual life. He was editor of the *Nouvelle Revue Française* from 1925 to 1940, and under his direction it became the most influential literary journal of interwar France. Among the authors he encouraged, edited, and published are Antonin Artaud, Jean-Paul Sartre, and Albert Camus. A writer in his own right, Paulhan received the Grand Prix de Littérature of the Académie Française in 1951 and was elected to the Académie Française in 1963.

JENNIFER BAJOREK is a lecturer in cultural studies at Goldsmiths, University of London, and has translated work by Sarah Kofman and Jacques Derrida.

CHARLOTTE MANDELL has translated work by Maurice Blanchot, Jean-Luc Nancy, Jean Genet, and Jacques Rancière, among others.

ERIC TRUDEL is an assistant professor of French at Bard College and is the author of *La Terreur à l'oeuvre: Théorie, poétique et éthique chez Jean Paulhan.*

The University of Illinois Press
is a founding member of the
Association of American University Presses.

Composed in 10.5/13.5 Minion Pro
with Minion Pro display
at the University of Illinois Press
Designed by Dennis Roberts
Index prepared by
Dylan Byers and Eric Trudel
Manufactured by Thomson-Shore, Inc.

University of Illinois Press
1325 South Oak Street
Champaign, IL 61820-6903
www.press.uillinois.edu